POSTNEGRITUDE VISUAL
AND LITERARY CULTURE

THE SUNY SERIES

CULTURAL STUDIES IN CINEMA / VIDEO

Edited by Wheeler Winston Dixon

POSTNEGRITUDE VISUAL AND LITERARY CULTURE

Mark A. Reid

STATE UNIVERSITY OF NEW YORK PRESS

Published by
State University of New York Press, Albany

© 1997 State University of New York

Printed in the United States of America

For information, address State University of New York Press,
State University Plaza, Albany, N.Y., 12246

For permission to reprint excerpts from their works, I am grateful to the
following individuals and/or publishers: Bob Kaufman, *Solitudes
Crowded with Loneliness.* © 1965 by Bob Kaufman. Reprinted by
permission of New Directions Publishing Corp.; and Jean Toomer,
"Brown River, Smile" in Yale Collection of American Literature,
Beinecke Rare Book and Manuscript Library, Yale University. Reprinted
by premission of Beinecke Rare Book and Manuscript Library, Yale
University; and "Oct. 5th, 1963" and "Believe, Believe" by Bob
Kaufman are from *Cranial Guitar*, Gerald Nicosia, editor, Coffee
House Press, 1996. © 1996 by the Estate of Bob Kaufman. Reprinted
by permission of Coffee House Press.

Production by Cathleen Collins
Marketing by Theresa Abad Swierzowski

Library of Congress Cataloging in Publication Data

Reid, Mark (Mark A.)
    PostNegritude visual and literary culture / Mark A. Reid.
        p. cm. — (SUNY series, cultural studies in cinema/video)
    Includes bibliographical references and index.
    ISBN 0-7914-3301-3 (hardcover : alk. paper). — ISBN 0-7914-3302-1
(pbk. : alk. paper)
    1. Blacks and mass media. I. Title. II. Series.
P94.5.B55R45   1997
305.8'96073—dc20   96-20292
                                                    CIP

10 9 8 7 6 5 4 3 2 1

To My Parents Who Were Always There

CONTENTS

ILLUSTRATIONS

ACKNOWLEDGMENTS

would like to thank the various audiences whose responses to my paper presentations have helped me to rethink the construction of blackness in much broader terms that connect with other identities held by people of African descent. I am indebted to the conference organizers for permitting me an audience who questioned my initial discussions about the postNegritude. I want to especially thank the organizers of the 1988 African Literature Discussion Group Section at the Modern Language Association Meeting, the 1990 Ohio University Film Conference, the 1992 Trajectories Symposium in Taipei, Taiwan, the 1993 ELAN conference in Lille, France, the 1993 American Studies Association Meeting, the 1993–1994 Society for Cinema Studies Conference, and most importantly, the Festival of PanAfrican Cinema and Television (FESPACO) in Ouagadougou, Burkina Faso. It is only through debates with friends, well-wishers and ardent critics that I have been able to organize my thoughts and write this book.

The University of Florida has been extremely helpful in supplying the necessary films (or should I say videos), equipment support, and research grants that helped me shape this more than eight-year research project into a book. My colleagues at Florida have offered interesting insights into various types of transracial and transnational cultural experiences. These chats in hallways, over lunch, and on the way to and from classes have fine tuned my understanding of the broader economic issues that sometimes determine issues of race and culture.

My thoughts on the postNegritude have been further shaped by a community of *Others* whose works and lived experiences in such places as Rwanda, Bosnia, and American inner cities require them to assimilate, negotiate, and sometimes, resist certain dehumanizing socioeconomic and psychological forces. Admittedly, I have borrowed ideas from the writings, conversations, and political actions of actional (as opposed to reactionary) scholars, artists, intellectuals, and persons outside these professions. Instead of an attempt to ceremonially name a recognizable coterie, I will remain silent and, thereby, equally honor them all.

I have tried to avoid recycling previously published essays. I think that I have been successful since, with the exception of my discussion of Rotimi Fani-Kayode black male nudes and Spike Lee's *Malcolm X*, I have not published the writings that are included in this book. Yet, as early as 1988, I presented a postNegritude analysis of two black literary works while a member on an MLA panel chaired by Sue Houchins and sponsored by the African Literatures Division. Since this date, I have discussed postNegritude at several professional meetings and in my published writings. Various editors, who shall also go unnamed but anonymously thanked, provided me with excuses to publish my thoughts about different postNegritude cultural products. I thank them for their editorial suggestions which I have incorporated in writing this book. I hope the essays, that now are bound together in this book, help those many marginalized *Others* continue the good fight for a postNegritude vision in real livable time, one that is inclusive and respectful of our multiple lived identities.

I also wish to express my gratitude to Bob Sharrad at City Lights Books, Sandra Kalagian at Coffee House Press, Dan Allman at New Directions Publishing Corporation, and Patricia Willis at Yale University Library.

Finally, I thank Clay Morgan and Cathleen Collins at SUNY Press, Wheeler Winston Dixon, the series editor of the series in which this book is published, and Kathleen League.

1

POSTNEGRITUDE AND CRITICAL THEORY

Affrican diasporic cultures wander through three major philo-sophical frames: the racial accommodation practiced by black conservatism, the middle-class appropriation represented by black liberalism, and the race-based resistance offered by black nation-alism. Certainly, all three philosophical positions are a response to the racism prevalent in American and European culture. Frantz Fanon refers to this type of cultural domination as *cultural imposition*. In discuss-ing the cultural imposition upon black Martinicans, Fanon remarks,

> Without turning to the idea of collective catharsis, it would be easy for me to show that, without thinking, the Negro selects himself as an object capable of carrying the burden of original sin. The white man chooses the black man for this function, and the black man who is white also chooses the black man. The black Antillean is the slave of this cultural imposition. After having been the slave of the white man, he enslaves himself. The Negro is in every sense of the word a victim of white civilization.[1]

Black conservative thought externally performs the function of the "black man who is white" and acquires certain social benefits from the white man who "chooses the black man" as his beast of burden. Booker T. Washington's politics of racial accommodation and Supreme Court

Justice Clarence Thomas's criticisms of affirmative action are examples of this exchange between blacks and whites.

The black descendants of African people who reside in Europe and the Americas are indicated by the terms Negro, black, and Afro-followed by the name of the country they inhabit. For example, I refer to the black people living in Britain as the "Afro-British," and I refer to blacks living in France as the "Afro-French." In using these terms, I am aware that there exist cultural differences between the Afro-British from Trinidad and those from Jamaica. I am also aware that the term African American collapses the cultural differences between black Americans of Haitian and those of Jamaican ancestry. I acknowledge their ethnic difference but I am also aware that their experiences of racism are common to blacks throughout the western world. Finally, the use of the terms "Negro" and "black" does not directly indicate any qualitative difference between the two terms. Racially hostile experience is what unites people of African ancestry. Yet and still, the experiences of class, ethnicity, sexuality, and religion constitute additional factors in the self-esteem of blackfolk. These extraracial factors create problems for a single definition of blackness as founded simply on race. This is especially true when race is not as static a term as one might wish to believe. Moreover, any analysis of black self-esteem must include considerations of the extraracial factors.

Fanon explains racial self-hatred as resulting from "cultural imposition" that produces blacks who racially objectify other blacks. According to Fanon, the Martinican's psychopathology (and, by correlation, that of any black of the diaspora) begins at a certain age when the West Indian recognizes that he embodies a black body but his collective unconscious (which is determined by the dominant European and or Anglo-American culture) equates the color black with an evil, careless, and bad-tempered nature. Fanon writes that, "Everything that is the opposite of these Negro modes of behavior is white. This must be recognized as the source of Negrophobia in the Antillean. In the collective unconscious, black = ugliness, sin, darkness, immorality. In other words, he is Negro who is immoral. If I order my life like that of a moral man, I simply am not a Negro."[2] This type of self-hatred appears simultaneously in reactionary, as opposed to actionable, forms of black conservatism, liberalism, and nationalism.

Fanon describes the dehumanizing racial elements of "cultural imposition" and shows how this is applicable to the cultural imposition of sexism, homophobia, classism, and ethnocentrism in European and American culture. I refer to these five elements—racism, sexism, homophobia, classism, and ethnocentrism—as the "destructive residue" of singular regimes of truth. A *postNegritude* analysis interprets the overlapping relationship between destructive residue and certain forms of black conservatism, liberalism, and nationalism. "PostNegritude" acts to subvert racism, sexism, and homophobia through womanist subversion of white and black patriarchal modes of production. It resists classism and ethnocentrism by affirming that black cultural identity is constantly unfolding to reveal its relationship to secular humanity.

This extended understanding of cultural imposition, then, recognizes the false threat of any "real white (or real black) man . . . waiting for me . . . (who) will tell me that it is not enough to try to be white (or black), but that white (or black) totality must be achieved."[3] Post-Negritude employs Fanon's nonbiological understanding of the collective unconscious which, according to Fanon, "is not dependent on cerebral heredity; it is the result of what I shall call the unreflected imposition of a culture."[4] Therefore, blacks and other similarly oppressed groups are not fated to view the world in one conventional manner.

The "postNegritude" project interprets essentialist and dualistic myths about whiteness and blackness, masculinity and femininity, heterosexuality and homosexuality, civilized and primitive as forms of a dying colonialism. The incumbent collective fears produced by these cultural myths transcend the boundaries from which these racial, gender, and sexual dualisms have their beginnings.[5]

Conservatism, liberalism, and nationalism coexist within the same world. They normally overlap and create contradictions. In black culture, their overlapping and coexistence create eruptions of funk and open spaces for various types of negotiations. For example, the rank-and-file politics of the black church exemplifies this conservative, liberal, and nationalist overlapping. This form of liberation politics tends to produce heterosexist, Christian, male-centered interpretations of the world. Surely, I acknowledge the importance of the African American church in assisting millions of blacks before and during the civil rights movement of the sixties. Furthermore, the Black church has produced such progressive black leaders as Jesse Jackson, Bishop Desmond Tutu, and Cornel West. Nonetheless, this institution has contained other liberation struggles.

In 1890s America, the politics of racial accommodation publicly accepted segregation in all its social, political, and cultural forms. From

1890 to 1915, Booker T. Washington was the most prominent black American leader because he was able to publicly promote racial segregation while he built the first black-directed trade school and privately fostered antisegregationist activities. Black accommodationist thought is a reaction to debilitating racial and social inequities that seem endless. Frantz Fanon describes the sociopsychical aspect of black accommodationist thought in this fashion:

> When the Negro makes contact with the white world, a certain sensitizing action takes place. If his psychic structure is weak, one observes a collapse of the ego. The black man stops behaving as an *actional* person. The goal of his behavior will be The Other (in the guise of the white man), for The Other alone can give him worth. That is on the ethical level: self-esteem.[6]

During periods of economic instability, racial accommodation becomes a strategy of survival for certain black Americans leaders. A recent marker of the perpetuation of racism by white policing forces has been registered in the videotaped beating of Rodney King by Los Angeles police officers. The Simi Valley jury's decision against prosecuting the white officers demonstrates the degree of racial injustice that prevails when a black man's human worth is determined by a jury of mostly white lower-middle-class suburbanites.

Yet and still, race is not the sole mediating factor in American judicial decisions. Supreme Court Justice Clarence Thomas, an African American and eminent conservative, won his appointment to the Supreme Court because of his race as well as his conservative legal opinion on abortion rights and affirmative action. Supreme Court Justice Thomas rejects the policy of affirmative action, even though such a policy could have prevented the existence of the predominantly white Simi Valley jury.

The Negro is contained within a white racist gaze as a nigger-object wherever (s)he goes. Therefore, and though I shiver at the racial dualism of this criticism, the racial and class differences between black Rodney King and the white Simi Valley policing jury are differences of primary importance. Such racial and class differences determine the (im)balance of American justice. The jury sanctioned the beating of Rodney King in finding the white Los Angeles police officers not guilty. Their verdict of not guilty reveals the permanence of institutional racism in American social life that never escapes the consciousness of the racial Other. The black Other recognizes racism's videotaped and ominous emergence as white cops and their guilty black suspect. The black Other hears their testimonies that are teeming with racial fears of blackness, its ugliness, its sin, its darkness and immorality. This dark messenger of ugliness threatened these white officers who have law in their side holsters, nightsticks in their hands, and the self-righteous support of a Simi Valley jury. This type of lawman is understood by the Simi Valley juries of this land. Their verdict is not a miscarriage of American justice but a direct result of it. Fanon is correct to point out that mental traumas occur when black racial Others meet with the policing agents of white patriarchy. Nonetheless, the racist practices of certain policing agents cannot determine encounters with blackfolk like Rodney King. Black survival is dependent on the appropriation and subversion of social injustices.

APPROPRIATING DOMINANT FORMS
AND ENTERING THE MIDDLE CLASS

Black progressive thought tends to appropriate and borrow from the traditions of American social-reform movements which, like the mainstream in the Abolitionist movement, stresses moderate social, political, and legal remedies for black social uplift. Rather than using the strategies of the black conservatives who publicly accept second-class citizenship while covertly struggling against racial discrimination, black progressives use judicial rulings to obtain and safeguard their civil rights.

In the beginning of the twentieth century, W. E. B. DuBois, a contemporary rival of Booker T. Washington, was the most important black intellectual to propose a liberal arts education for certain African Americans. DuBois argued that the "talented tenth" of the African American population would best prepare the remaining blacks for the responsibilities of full American citizenship. DuBois believed that educated blacks would return to their communities and become the politicians, teachers, and religious leaders of the black masses. The political writings of W. E. B. DuBois, the 1940–1960s court battles of the National Association for the Advancement of Colored People (NAACP), the 1960s Southern Christian Leadership Council, the Student Non-Violent Coordinating Committee (SNCC), and Jesse Jackson's "Rainbow Coalition" exemplify American reformism and black progressive thought. Similar to the interracial composition of the initial SNCC membership, the Rainbow Coalition consisted of a multiracial, multiethnic, and progressive constituency who sponsored Jesse Jackson's 1988 presidential campaign.

Similar to the developmental history of Asian American, Chicano, and Native American Studies, the African American Studies, commonly referred to as Black Studies, has had an ambiguous relationship with American consensus-oriented cultural paradigms. Regardless of the political and ideological merits of a national cultural-studies paradigm, black culture tends to resist being assimilated into any cultural-studies paradigm which ignores the importance of race, class, and gender. Moreover, this resistance is further increased by nonblack Americans who oppose their government's present (and former) suppression of democratic liberation movements in southern Africa, the Americas, and the Pacific rim.

Other differences between the two cultural-studies paradigms include the international scholarly interests of African American studies (also expressed in panAfricanism and black nationalism). Contrarily, American Studies applies a national perspective to study social and cultural phenomena within the United States. Another point of contention between the two includes the criticism that Americanists tend to use Euro-American norms and models formulated by the past and present white male arbiters of American culture. Initially, these Euro-American taste makers discerned the intellectual and aesthetic merit of black works based on Euro-American values. This predominance of Eurocentric models, if we limit ourselves to the discipline of American cultural studies, has all but changed with the development of such extra-American studies programs as Chicano/Chicana, Asian American, Native American, Jewish, Black, Women's, and Gay Studies. Now, many critics find that certain Africanist and Afro-Americanist scholarly works support forms of heterosexism, male chauvinism, ethnocentrism, racial essentialism, and anti-Semitism.

Furthermore, many African Americanists discuss the intellectual and aesthetic merits of black cultures in the Americas, Europe, and Africa by collapsing important ethnic and religious differences between and among these black communities. Now, and without fear of being labeled a racist, white Americanists can criticize Africanists and African Americanists of this additional ethnocentric folly since certain scholars make essentialist claims about culturally different black communities. Yet and still, the international black community meets with racial discrimination in Europe and the Americas. The experience of color discrimination, and the communality of the experience of racism, provides blacks with a tie that binds them with a victim-identity which in its nationalist and panAfricanist mode takes two forms—Negritude and "postNegritude." I will elaborate on the differences between the two forms later.

As early as the 1950s, Fanon cautioned against black essentialism but held that blackfolk are internationally despised and, therefore, the antiracist struggle and "Negro" identity is of primary importance to any black person regardless of their nationality. Fanon states,

> In the beginning I wanted to confine myself to the Antilles. But, regardless of consequences, dialectic took the upper hand and I was compelled to see that the Antillean is first of all a Negro. Nevertheless, it would be impossible to overlook the fact that there are Negroes whose nationality is Belgian, French, English; there are also Negro republics. How can one claim to have gotten hold of an essential when such facts as these demand one's recognition? The truth is that the Negro race has been scattered, that it can no longer claim unity. . . . In the universal situation of the Negro there is ambiguity, which is, however, resolved in his concrete existence. . . . Against all the arguments I have just cited, I come back to one fact: Wherever he goes, the Negro remains a Negro.[7]

Negritude describes the international movement of black cultural and political production from the 1920s to the present while "post-Negritude" is an extension of this movement to encompass other identities which blackfolk may share with nonblacks.[8]

Before continuing with this discussion, I hope that my criticism of Negritude is not misunderstood as a total rejection of this movement. The criticism expresses an earnest *desire* for Negritude to realize that black cultural

> [i]dentity is not as transparent or unproblematic as we think. Perhaps instead of thinking of identity as an already accomplished fact, which the new cultural practices then represent, we should think, instead, of identity as a "production," which

is never complete, always in process, and always constituted within, not outside, representation. This view problematises the very authority and authenticity to which the term, "cultural identity," lays claim.[9]

In returning to the damaging effects of Eurocentric cultural criticism, one must remember that historical duration affects and limits the degree of empowerment of any "truth" regime. When one ignores the transient quality of "truth," one also ignores the ever-changing and fluid characteristics of certain empowered whites and their indeterminate relationship with multinational capitalism and its processes of "cultural imposition." Such a move would also ignore those Others who have never been *directly* empowered by the macroregimes of cultural production. In commenting on systems that establish universal interests, Pierre Bourdieu offers a set of questions which one should consider before proposing such universalizing norms. He asks,

> Who has an interest in the universal? Or rather: what are the social conditions that have to be fulfilled for certain agents to have an interest in the universal? How are fields created such that agents, in satisfying their particular interests, contribute thereby to producing the universal . . . ? Or fields in which agents feel obliged to set themselves up as defenders of the universal (such as the intellectual field in certain national traditions. . .)? In short, in certain fields, at a certain moment and for a certain time (that is, in a nonreversible way), there are agents who have an interest in the universal.[10]

In the sixties, the dominant paradigm of American identity fractured when the civil rights movement and black nationalism demanded a reformulation of the American values and norms. Blacks, womanists, feminists, and other equally marginal groups questioned the myths and symbols of the not-so-great white patriarchal leaders. Historically, American culture has maintained racially separate and economically unequal places for its nonwhite and female citizens. Now, these groups reject their positions of silence, invisibility, and unimportance.

Generally, white middle-class male academics established programs to study American norms and values. Though they had honest intentions when constructing the American mind as a national identity, these men were agents of their class position, race, and gender. The founders of American cultural studies, with few exceptions, were white middle-class males who busily attacked the European hegemony in the American liberal arts education. Blinded by their ideological goals, they explained post-WWII American culture by their subjective visions. Quite understandably, a new and racially mixed generation of American intellectuals refuted and reformed the existing interpretive claims, all of which offended many of the older generation of white, male guardians of post-WWII culture. The status quo held that the liberalism which now reigned in the academy was their doing, and they, therefore, could not be guilty of ethnocentrism, sexism, and other crimes against the academy. The more rigid patricians held that debate must be civil and their patriarchal myths and values must not be subverted. The consensus family order must not be divorced of its heterosexual, Euro-American male discursive norms. Black nationalists appropriated the patriarchal discourse of their brothers and attacked its Eurocentric myths. White feminists followed and appropriated the Eurocentric paradigm of their lovers, brothers, and father, and then attacked their sexism. Womanists and feminists of color subverted both racial and androcentric hegemonies while their gay brothers and lesbian sisters combined the progressive elements of the black nationalists and white feminists to disrupt the hegemony of heterosexual ways of being. All of these critical processes, if taken together, damaged the unquestioned legitimacy of whiteness, maleness, and heterosexuality.

Black American culture, like other racially borderline cultures, grew separate from, but in many psychological ways similar to, the white American mainstream. In describing the cultural tension between celebrating ethnic difference and affirming an American identity, Asian American scholar Elaine H. Kim notes,

> So much writing by Asian Americans is focused on the theme of claiming an American, as opposed to Asian, identity that we may begin to wonder if this constitutes accommodation, a collective colonized spirit—the fervent wish to "hide our ancestry," which is impossible for us anyway, to relinquish our marginality, and to lose ourselves in an intense identification with the hegemonic culture. Or is it in fact a celebration of our marginality and a profound expression of protest against being defined by domination?[11]

Kim underlines the ambiguity that reigns in the un-meltable lives of non-European Americans. Consequently, black intellectuals and artists portray their criticisms of mainstream American culture in a conspicuously racial manner yet they argue for opportunities to participate in a reformulated mainstream America. Their criticisms celebrate marginality, otherness, and difference. Exhibiting the simultaneity present in most "postNegritude" processes,[12] this form of criticism is a profound protest against white patriarchal standards. Black creativity explores the arbitrary relationship that blacks have not only with America but also with black patriarchal forms which have not yet dismantled their own subsystems of cultural imposition. Consequently, certain blacks face double and triple alienation from both the black and white communities. In his autobiography *Bourgeois Blues*, Jake Lamar describes an instance of this dilemma of an embattled double consciousness:

> By the end of my first semester, I felt as if I were in a social limbo. I avoided getting linked to any clique, but every time I passed the black tables without taking a seat, I felt a twinge of guilt, as if I were breaking some rule, betraying some obligation. . . . The breezy cordiality I displayed with most everyone masked the growing anger I felt. I was angry at all the people, white and black, whom I saw as small-minded, bigoted and shallow. And I was angry at myself, for while all I wanted was to be accepted as myself, I feared that the self I cherished so much was terminally ambivalent.[13]

Unfortunately, certain types of antiracist criticisms inadvertently sustain the racial dualism that European colonizers used to rationalize their imperialistic intrusions in Africa, Asia, and the Americas. Additionally, if marginal and borderline groups merely focus on single identity issues such as race, their efforts will conceal the extraracial issues of class, gender, and sexual orientation.

Until recently, black-oriented cultural-studies paradigms glossed over issues of gender, class, and sexual orientation. As stated earlier, debates over the construction of black identity can no longer sustain Negritude's previously one-dimensional racial definition of Africa and its black European and black American diasporas. The "postNegritude" view of "Africa" refuses the image of an idyllic country of black primitives who evaded European cultural imposition. "PostNegritude" reasoning and creativity are processes which realize that

The original 'Africa' is no longer there. It too has been transformed. History is, in that sense, irreversible. We must not collude with the West which, precisely, normalises and appropriates Africa by freezing it into some timeless zone of the primitive, unchanging past. Africa must at last be reckoned with by . . . (black diasporic) people, but it cannot in any simple sense by merely recovered.

It belongs irrevocably, for us, to what Edward Said once called an 'imaginative geography and history', which helps 'the mind to intensify its own sense of itself by dramatising the difference between what is close to it and what is far away'. . . . Our belongingness to it constitutes what Benedict Anderson calls 'an imagined community'. To *this* 'Africa', which is a necessary part of the (black diasporic) . . . imaginary, we can't literally go home again.[14]

Thus, the end of Negritude and the beginning of "postNegritude" indicates a historical shift in black thinking about Africa, black cultural production, and the political effects of nomadic multinational corporations. These factors and other extra-racial phenomena determine the psychological identity and socioeconomic conditions of any community. These factors also limit the historical moment that any marginal and borderline entity negotiates across racial, ethnic, class, sexual, and ideological boundaries.

BLACK NATIONALISM AS A FORM OF CULTURAL RESISTANCE

Black nationalism is a third philosophical form that remains important to any discussion of black cultural studies and the idea of "post-Negritude" and "womanism." In its most progressive manifestations it is a form of political and economic resistance that aligns itself with other progressive forms of political and economic resistance. As a political and cultural movement, black nationalism acknowledges the interconnected historical experiences of black communities in Europe, the Americas, and Africa.

The culture of the African diaspora includes concrete and particular experiences of black people after their physical removal from Africa. Their experiences include the overlapping of African cultures and

European cultures, and thereby create black cultures that are neither purely African nor purely European. In fact, there are no pure European cultures. The idea of nation-state identity is based on an imagined singular wholeness and artificial national borders. One need only to witness the ethnic warfare in what was formerly Yugoslavia and the ongoing civil strife in various African nations.

The creolization of the black diaspora (the racial and cultural mixing of people) is an unarguable fact. Still, many members of this diaspora view the continent of Africa as their spiritual source and the home of their ancestors. The cultural production and politics of this type of consciousness are black nationalism and panAfricanism, which remain important tools but have their drawbacks. In the above, I quoted Stuart Hall's comment on the problems of one-dimensional identity, which is "not as transparent or unproblematic as we think." Hall suggests that identity is always in a process of becoming. Thus, identity is always incompleteness, and according to Hall, "[t]his view problematises the very authority and authenticity to which the term, 'cultural identity,' lays claim."[15] Any theory that acknowledges "the becomingness of blackness" evokes a "postNegritude" understanding of black cultural identity. Black nationalism and panAfricanism, in their most progressive narrative forms, stress a "becomingness of a blackness" that has not yet arrived. Only in this narrative form are nationalism and panAfricanism a part of a "postNegritude" which is the "play" located between two different spaces. The "post" in "postNegritude" denotes a second phase of previous forms of Negritude and panAfricanism,

> [a] second, related but different view of cultural identity. This second position recognises that, as well as the many points of similarity, there are also critical points of deep and significant difference which constitute 'what we really are'; or rather—since history has intervened—'what we have become'. . . . Cultural identity, in this second sense, is a matter of 'becoming' as well as 'being'. . . . It is not something that already exists, transcending place, time, history and culture. Cultural identities come from somewhere, have histories. But, like everything which is historical, they undergo constant transformation. Far from being eternally fixed in some essentialist past, they are subject to the continuous 'play' of history, culture and power. . . . Identities are the names we give to the

different ways we are positioned by, and position ourselves within, the narratives of the past.[16]

This form of black nationalism and panAfricanism is evident in black visual art. Black films such as Julie Dash's *Daughters of the Dust* (1991) and Spike Lee's *Jungle Fever* (1991) use narrative and filmic devices that call forth both Negritude and postNegritude sensibilities. The postNegritude is also apparent in the negotiation between black masculinity and black gay identity in the visual works of Marlon Riggs and Rotimi Fani-Kayode. It is visible in Gordon Parks's FSA "Charwoman" photographs that indicate tension between Black and American identity. PostNegritude visual construction permeates Adrian Piper's mixed-media collages that speak of the arbitrariness of her racial identity.

PostNegritude is also discernible in black literature. For instance, such 1960s novels as John A. Williams's *The Man Who Cried I Am* and Ayi Kwei Armah's *Fragments*, Adrienne Kennedy's absurdist play *The Funnyhouse of a Negro*, and Bob Kaufman's poetry dramatize psychological tensions that arise when Negritude and postNegritude identity paradigms meet during the literary hegemony of Negritude aesthetics.

APPROPRIATION, NEGOTIATION, AND RESISTANCE

Neither black conservatism, liberalism, nor nationalism express pure forms of appropriation, negotiation, and resistance to mainstream Euro-American culture. Black culture develops within and around the competing tensions created by the intermittent desire to appropriate, negotiate, and resist mainstream American and European cultures. Since the late sixties, Black Studies has negotiated its place within American and European universities. Similar to any other academic discipline, its leading spokespersons, such as Houston Baker at the University of Pennsylvania, Hazel Carby at Yale, and Henry Louis Gates and Cornel West at Harvard, employ elements of appropriation, negotiation, and resistance to safeguard a space for black cultural studies within the American academy. Each of these scholars directs a Black Studies program at a predominantly white institution. The alliance between the black scholar and the white university as well as between these black scholars and nonblack scholars is of a political nature. This is especially true when one considers the European origins of these four elite universities and the general marginality of black studies in the academy.

The marginal space of black cultural studies in educational institutions does not permit its black scholars to avoid theoretical questions. In fact, black communities who experience socioeconomic and psychic processes of racial discrimination demand the formulation of theoretical explanations. They also demand practical ways of resisting these destructive processes. Any serious theory of black resistance should consider the nonessentialist writings of Frantz Fanon, Stuart Hall, and womanists. In form and application, theories of resistance should attempt to explain the interrelationship of processes of racism and macrocosmic processes of ethnic, sexual, and religious bigotry.

Pierre Bourdieu states that "in every field . . . there is a struggle for a monopoly of legitimacy."[17] The "struggle for a monopoly of legitimacy" should not pit advocates of panAfricanism and black nationalism against those Others who are equally victimized. Professor Barbara Christian, the former chair of the Afro-American Studies Department at the University of California at Berkeley, underscores the problems of this struggle. In criticizing the race for legitimacy by black academics, she writes,

> My major objection to the race for theory . . . really hinges on the question, 'for whom are we doing what we are doing when we do literary criticism?' It is . . . the central question today especially for the few of us who have infiltrated the academy enough to be wooed by it. The answer to that question determines what orientation we take in our work, the language we use, the purposes for which it is intended.[18]

In response to Christian's question I offer "postNegritude" as a tentative answer. The root of a postNegritude aesthetics is founded upon a womanist ideology which is similar to Michele Wallace's description of black feminism. Wallace writes that it is

> [a] socialist feminism, not yet fully formulated, whose primary goal is a liberatory and profound (almost necessarily nonviolent) political transformation. Second, I assume as well that black feminist creativity, to the extent that its formal and commercial qualities will allow, is inherently critical of current oppressive and repressive political, economic and social arrangements affecting not just black women but black people as a group.[19]

The language of the "postNegritude" inevitably appropriates certain theoretical notions without totally relying on their paradigms. The root of the "postNegritude" is the psychical and sociocultural history of postcolonialism. A "postNegritude" orientation appropriates nonessentialist ideas and negotiates a sociopsychic space which acknowledges

> [t]hat *race* functions to constitute concrete individuals as white and black. Here the movement from subjects to men and women, to black and white, not only 'marks the conceptual distance between two orders of discourse, the discourse of philosophy or political theory and the discourse of reality,' it marks the conceptual distance of race and the race-oriented forms of popular culture.[20]

Yet, this sociopsychic racial space resists the colonizing urge to find legitimacy in the arms of static theoretical and political discourses of racial and sexual essentialism. "PostNegritude" wants to bring the videotaped beating of Rodney King into the churches of white middle-class America — the Simi Valley of the American racial mind.

THE MICROSTRUGGLES AND
MINIPOLITICS OF POSTNEGRITUDE

The growth of any paradigm is measured by its ability to maintain its canon and lessen the destructive effects of dissent by those exterior texts and discourses that would usurp its rules and beliefs. Black Studies has always been a marginal discipline within the academy. It has also sustained its place within the academy by appropriating, negotiating, and resisting those other essentialist texts and discourses that threaten the unity of one black voice.

Recently, black feminists, gays, and lesbians have expressed critical paradigms that synthesize racial and extraracial issues. It is their advancement of this synthesis that rejuvenates the present debate in black cultural studies. The "minority discourses" of these doubly and sometimes triply victimized members deny the initial assumptions of Negritude, black nationalism, and panAfricanism — black cultural identity. The extraracial concerns of these three groups expand the meaning of blackness and create diversity where racial stagnation and fraud once reigned. "PostNegritude" shifts reveal the rich polyphony that has always existed in black culture.

Before I discuss these minority voices of a racial minority community, I should like to refer to the cautionary words of Caren Kaplan, a first-world feminist critic. In commenting on feminist criticism, she provides a womanist understanding of the political nature of the "post-Negritude" project that I am describing. Kaplan writes,

> The first stage in this process is refusing the privilege of universalizing theories. Some of us may experience ourselves as minor in a world that privileges the masculine gender. But our own centrality in terms of race, class, ethnicity, religious identity, age, nationality, sexual preference, and levels of disabilities is often ignored in our own work. All women are not equal, and we do not have the same experiences. . . . When we insist upon gender alone as a universal system of explanation we sever ourselves from other women. How can we speak to each other if we deny our particularities?[21]

Kaplan underscores the arbitrary nature of minority and majority status for white women. Her comments are also relevant for people of color whose gender, class, ethnicity, nationality, and sexual orientation may afford them privileges over others like them. All people of color are not equal. We do not have the same experiences. Thus, we must avoid universalizing race, class, and postcolonial subjectivity, and acknowledge our particularities as we learn to speak of our similarities.

Kaplan also warns feminist critics against repeating forms of imperialism. She writes, "First world feminist criticism is struggling to avoid repeating the same imperialist moves that we claim to protest. We must leave home, as it were, since our homes are often sites of racism, sexism, and other damaging social practices."[22] Black critics should consider her advice when writing on the constitution of black culture, black identity, and black theory. Critics who desire a world in which racial dualism, ethnocentrism, and nationalism have lost their currency, must avoid the same imperialism and racism that enslaves and dehumanizes third-world people, though they may live in first-world metropolises in Europe, the Americas, and Australia.

In the chapters that follow, I will discuss how certain visual and literary works dramatize black history as well as introduce *invention* in the construction of black cultural identity. I will borrow from the works of Frantz Fanon, Stuart Hall, and certain womanist critics (women and men) to argue that many of these creative works express the understanding that

> [t]here is no white world, there is no white ethic, any more than there is a white intelligence. There are in every part of the world (wo)men who search. I am not a prisoner of history. I should not seek there for the full meaning of my destiny. I should constantly remind myself that the real *leap* consists in introducing invention into existence. In the world through which I travel, I am endlessly creating myself.[23]

Part of my concern thus far has been to discuss how negotiation and resistance occur when Negritude and postNegritude paradigms meet at the crossroads of the becoming of blackness. Additionally, I have analyzed the sociopsychic effects of the unreflected imposition of ethnocentric cultural paradigms.[24]

In the following chapters I move from a description of postNegritude to an interpretive application of its principles. In doing so, I discuss and critically analyze the artistic processes that permit minority discourses within certain black diasporic and African communities. As I suggested above, "postNegritude" represents a reconstructed black philosophy of cultural identity and cultural production. The following chapters analyze how marginal and borderline people of African ancestry use the visual and literary arts to scrutinize monolithic forms of black subjectivity. Their works inscribe womanist, gay, lesbian, and interracial experiences into the constitution of black culture and black identity.

SUMMARIZING THE COMPONENTS OF POSTNEGRITUDE

Some readers may perceive, albeit incorrectly, that I offer different kinds of definitions of *postNegritude*. To avoid this confusion, I will summarize postNegritude's various components. First, I will list a few of the varied *tensions* that provide free zones in which *postNegritude actions* might occur.

The recently televised spectacles like the Anita Hill-Clarence Thomas hearings, the videotaped Rodney King beating, the Simi Valley jury's not-guilty decision, the urban revolt following the Simi Valley verdict, the O.J. Simpson trial and the jury's not-guilty judgment, provide some of the crucial raw materials that produce debates about "race card" justice in America. These debates and reactions create *post-Negritude tensions* and provide free zones for possible *postNegritude actions*. These spectacles about lived experiences, however, should never be taken as the postNegritude in and of itself. The Hill-Thomas, Rodney King, Simi Valley, O.J. Simpson episodes increase the already present tensions of race, gender, class, and religion. These social tensions might then percolate into postNegritude actions through creative, revelatory, and political processes.

For example the Hill-Thomas hearings brought to the national forefront how diversified is black political thought on the civil right movement's legacy and sexual harassment in the workplace. The hearing revealed, to popular audiences, the existence of an articulate and conservative group of African Americans who had been previously unknown to this audience, and ignored by both black and nonblack liberals. Anita Hill, not Clarence Thomas, created the necessary postNegritude tensions that opened, revealed, and exposed the many free zones in which postNegritude acts can occur. Throughout this work, I will repeatedly list various *components of postNegritude*, so as not to confuse the reader with *postNegritude tensions* that give rise to the possibility of *postNegritude actions*.

PostNegritude acts constitute any effort to challenge hegemonies of power through critical analysis (as this book outlines), through social action (as followed the Anita Hill-Clarence Thomas hearings), and through the creative imagination (as present in some of the visual and literary works discussed in this book). PostNegritude, then, creates, reveals, and exposes the nonessential nature of socially constructed ideas about race, gender, class, and nation. The community that supported Hill's right to publicize Thomas's alleged sexual harassment serves to *create* a womanist postNegritude. The extension of Hill's experience to speak for and about all women *and* men who are sexually harassed in the workplace *reveals* the nonessentialist actional processes of any postNegritude act. Further analysis of the Hill-Thomas hearings exposes the many languages that postNegritude can speak to issues beyond the oneness of race, gender, class, and nation in the black and nonblack communities.

So, black conservative political voices interrupt the hegemony of liberalism in the black community and provide a dialogic space, a free zone for *Other* voices to speak and act. A professional African American woman, such as the Yale-educated lawyer Anita Hill, provides a precedence for other black conservative women who might normally be silenced by their own conservative politics and/or professional realities.

In this book, I do not discuss how postNegritude analysis applies to the O.J. Simpson trial but I will comment on it briefly here. The American media constructed the O.J. Simpson trial as another B movie-cum-telefilm of a courtroom drama. The trial's news coverage brought the issues of class, interracial intimacy, and multinational capitalism to another level of mediocrity. The jury's not-guilty verdict provided the necessary postNegritude tensions to filter through America's medi(a)ocre strainer. The jury's not-guilty verdict, like Hill's accusation, created an American entertainment-industry Frankenstein-like monster—The O.J. Simpson Jury. Nonblack liberals revealed some very hideous racist traits. Most, but not all, African Americans were not shocked by these revelations and, in a very postNegritude utterance, acknowledged this to mainstream media. Basically, they said that their sociopolitical lives had not greatly changed since the fifties. They admitted that there had only been a reshuffling of the individual players (the black middle class). Still, "race card" determinants defined who among the American middle classes became fat and who remained comfortably lean, and what classes were totally out of the picture frame—the poor and working poor. For instance, as I recall, the white female lawyer, not her black male colleague, receives the most lucrative multimillion-dollar book contract. This reality and the fact that both public prosecutors stubbornly relied on the testimony of Mark Furman, a racist policeman, reveals the systemic business-as-usual racism that the media and most of the public mistakenly identify as a singular "race card" meted out by one all too powerful black lawyer—Johnnie Cochran. PostNegritude revelation uses this fissure to utter that "the whole deck is a history of race-card dealings with all people of color, not just with one black rich O.J. Simpson." PostNegritude does not make villains of individuals who are produced by an inhumane system. PostNegritude thinking humanizes the individual and states, "It is the system, not the individual cops such as Mark Furman or publicity-hungry lawyers like Johnnie Cochran, who load the deck and deal the cards." Therefore, the tragic fall of an American sports hero, the issue of interracial marriage and biracial children, and the rumors of an impending interracial marriage between the dream-team lawyers are all possible postNegritude tensions but they become mere hyperbole that obscures the "race card" realpolitik. Ironically, the jury's verdict was mostly affected by classism (O.J.'s wealth afforded him the best legal team), racism (O.J.'s interracial marriage provoked Mark Furman), and sexism since O.J. physically abused Nicole.

The O.J. Simpson trial marks, after the Hill-Thomas hearings, the second time within a five-year period that white liberals squared-off with the majority of the middle, working, and poor classes in the Black community. These are postNegritude times that create *tensions* that do not guarantee postNegritude creations, revelations, and expositions of the nonessential nature of race, gender, class and nation.

These very popular spectacles of postNegritude *tensions*, like the Hill-Thomas hearings, resemble serialized B films that are available to the largest popular audience—the television viewer. If the reader will permit my stretching the definition of a film genre, these B courtroom dramas evoke popular sentiment that is far from being postNegritudinal in kind, but may, however, create postNegritude tensions and free zones for dialogic occasions as illustrated in the proliferation of radio-television talk shows and nonacademic and scholarly essays and books commenting on the Hill-Thomas hearings and the O.J. Simpson trial. Again, they do not create examples of the postNegritude. The postNegritude *tensions* produce free zones for postNegritude actional politics as illustrated in the actional exchanges between Michael Lerner and Cornel West.[25]

I have not exhausted the list of postNegritude's many components, but postNegritude should not be confused with the various tensions and opportunities that occur and call forth a postNegritude action.

2

NEGRITUDE TO
POSTNEGRITUDE

nternationally, Eurocentric patriarchy and racism affect the economic and social livelihood of black people. Together, patriarchal and racist practices support new forms of colonialism in the African diaspora. For instance, in contemporary America, Eurocentric processes produce such racist acts as the beating of Rodney King and the mainstream media's depiction of black communities as solely a narrative of drive-by shootings, drugs, and car-jackings. On a sociopsychic level, these processes generate such racist images as the Republican Party use of Willy Horton during the 1988 United States presidential campaign.

Because the descendants of white Europeans have usually authorized and commissioned these and other racist images and acts against people of African ancestry, a few black nationalists, to resist racism, have formulated racially essentialist explanations. They say that these acts reflect the innately racist nature of all whites.

Contrary to these findings, racism and its victimized object has little to do with the genetic structure of any particular race of human beings. Racism and bigotry are profitable enterprises, and any sensible antiracist struggle that borrows the essentialist claims of its enemy, will increase the authority of such racist propositions and give these prejudices a more inflated currency. Antiracist strategies must work to bankrupt the currency of racist projects whenever they appear. Analysis should explain why these beliefs and actions are disadvantageous to the economic and social health of a nation, community, and individual, regardless of their degree of victimization. Instead of explaining racism as an essentially "white thing," it would be more productive to view it as a sociopsychic problem that is generally aided by patriarchal conventions and values which sustain a multinational corporate economy.

No, I do not think that any actual communist state has escaped racist and sexist practices. Yes, I am aware of past and present ethnic strife in parts of black Africa and what was formerly Yugoslavia. Nonetheless, I cannot ignore how multinational corporations export racist and patriarchal images throughout their markets. Moreover, I concede that any *economic* solution to racist and sexist processes of cultural production must negotiate with the capitalist needs of multinational corporations.

Notwithstanding the importance of studying the macroeconomic effects of multinational capitalism on culture, this study is more interested in how art portrays the sociopsychic and economic fears of people in the grips of social and psychological change. These people include certain whites and certain men, as well as particular blacks and particular women, who must relinquish their positions within a racist patriarchal system. The postNegritude is more adapted to the interpretation of the imaginary depiction of this latter challenge—the analysis of an interracial and transgendered group and the dramatization of their sociopsychic and economic investment in racism and patriarchy.

Hopefully, as postNegritude negotiates a hybrid space in the popular imagination, this negotiation will have some bearing on the cultural products made and distributed by multinational corporations. Here, negotiation is not "selling-out," it is appropriating a dominant form for subversive purposes. As the critic Homi K. Bhabha explains,

> Negotiation is what politics is all about. . . . Subversion is negotiation; transgression is negotiation; negotiation is not just some kind of compromise or 'selling out' which people too easily understand it to be. . . . Political negotiation is a very important issue, and hybridity is precisely about the fact that when a new situation, a new alliance formulates itself, it may demand that you should translate your principles, rethink them, extend them.[1]

In applying Bhabha's general understanding of negotiation and hybridity, I argue for a postNegritude understanding of race and cultural identity as a socially acquired and unfixed process rather than a biological fact. Racist thinkers use notions of "race" and "cultural identity" to explain what they allege are the fundamental differences between whites and blacks. In arguing against racial essentialism, Frantz Fanon argues that "the collective unconscious, without having to fall back on the genes, is purely and simply, the sum of prejudices, myths, collective attitudes of a given group. . . . [T]he collective unconscious is cultural, which means acquired."² Thus, the degree of melanin in either the white oppressor or black victim is not the postNegritude's explanation of racism. In the postNegritude, the color of one's skin has no immediate relationship with either their political ideology or their possible production of a cultural identity. Through sociological processes, one usually identifies with a particular nation, racial group, and local community. Nations, races, and local communities are always becoming and unbecoming something that they never intended to be. For instance, in the United States, there have been black mayors of large cities, there has been a black governor of Virginia and black commander-in-chief of the United States armed forces, and there is an ultra-conservative black Supreme Court Justice. There have always been children of racially, ethnically, and religiously mixed parents. Blacks and whites are "far from being eternally fixed in some essentialist past."

Undoubtedly, European cultural hegemony has internationally objectified the black African Other. I, however, still maintain that the articulation of racist forms of patriarchy does not necessarily translate into the racial and gender physiognomy of the white male who might directly benefit from racist impositions of patriarchal culture. In a published interview, black womanist poet June Jordan stresses the need for building transgendered bridges to combat rape and other forms of patriarchy. In responding to womanist filmmaker Pratibha Parmar, Jordan states,

> In order to eliminate the possibility of rape or even the likelihood of rape for women generally we have to go beyond ourselves. We have to sit down with and/or stand up to and finally in some way impact upon men. I don't think it's ever enough on your own.³

Echoing Homi Bhabha's earlier discussion of the importance of political negotiation, Jordan argues for a postNegritude antisexist struggle that is able to negotiate and resist. She also alludes to the need to safeguard an openness for the inclusion of males. In the same interview, Jordan finds that any serious black struggle against racism must include whites. She adds,

> And I would say the same thing about race identity politics. I didn't, nor did my people or my parents, invent the problems that we as black people have to solve. We black people, the victims of racism are not the ones that have to learn new ways of thinking about things so that we can stop racist habits of thought. Neither do we have the power to be placed in appropriate situations to abolish the social and economic arrangements that have assured the continuity of racism in our lives. That's for white people.[4]

Unlike most current forms of Negritude, postNegritude negotiation and resistance is not necessarily linked to the racial and gender physiognomy of the individual or group who might utter a womanist, antiracist articulation or be honored by such a postNegritude utterance. Post-Negritude politics realizes "that in any particular political struggle, new sites are always being opened up, and if you keep referring those new sites to old principles, then you are not actually able to participate in them fully and productively and creatively."[5]

There are two poignant illustrations of postNegritude as a social phenomenon. One example is the white Latin American man who videotaped the Los Angeles officers' beating of Rodney King and sent it to a local news station. This act represents a postNegritude act of resistance. Another example of postNegritude *actional* resistance is the group of blacks who, during the Los Angeles uprising, stopped reactionary blacks from beating the white truck driver Reginald Denny.

PostNegritude processes, as mentioned earlier, are actional and resist through negotiation. Negritude processes are often reactions to racism and, sometimes, appropriate certain sociopsychic elements of the Eurocentric patriarchal culture. I will now address the sociopsychic function of racist imagery in American popular culture and, later, I will discuss how black-oriented media negotiates and resists these racist and patriarchal visual constructions.

Beginning with D.W. Griffith's infamous cinematic masterpiece *Birth of A Nation* (1915), through such Civil War epics as *Gone With the Wind* (1939) and, half a century later, *Glory* (1989), American film studios have consistently depicted southern race relations as a static exchange of black flesh between northern and southern white men. White men are invariably characterized as southern villains or northern saviors. This immobile black and white image frames the filmic portrait of black southern life and its relationship to white patriarchs.

Generally, plantation melodramas articulate sexuality on two different levels. The first level confines white southern women, with the exception of her birthing white babies, to a dispassionate life. Conversely, it forces black women into a demeaning life of satiating the carnal desires of white men as well as being one of the primary vehicles for the reproduction of slavery. Most plantation melodramas characterize black women as alternating between maidservants to their white mistress and the subdued rape victim of their white master. Both black and white women, however, are determined by this patriarchal narrative that enforces white nationalism and female passivity. For example, Richard Fleischer's *Mandingo* (1970) reveals how slavery dehumanizes both the white female and the black slave community. In southern plantation films like *Mandingo*, the black woman is cinematically framed as the all-encompassing womb of servitude to the carnal and economic needs of white patriarchy; she is the unwilling recipient of the southern planter's seed.

Furthermore, this system objectifies black men as brainless studs who exist solely for the production of slaves. Racist patriarchal codes determine the form and content of black masculinity. The system either emasculates or creates oversexed black men. Like the white master, the oversexed black male is a violent brute who lacks paternal interests in his black children or romantic feelings toward his wife. He is very much like the white master in yet another way; the oversexed black man, different from his emasculated brother, shares a general rapacious appetite for women outside his race. This system enacts laws to control the *imagined* sexual appetite of the black man; similar laws, however, are unnecessary for the protection of black female slaves. The black woman's body provides the institution of slavery with its future workers and provides white masters with an outlet for carnal pleasures that the system forbids its white women. According to the generic requirements, any sexualized black man must simulate docility when in the presence of representatives of white patriarchy. When a black man is incapable of showing deference to the white man, he will suffer a lynching, or a beating (witness the beating of Rodney King).

Psychologically, the lynching and rape of the sexualized black man and woman express white patriarchal desires to physically consume, psychologically suppress, and historically fix the black man's phallus and the black woman's womb. Black empowerment is imagined as both an erotic and political threat to white patriarchy. When these threats seem more real than imagined, certain members of the black community suffer beatings, rapes, burnings, and castrations. Mainstream media and popular art offer socially accepted ways to mentally expunge the fear of black empowerment. The northern black Other has escaped the fixity of racist southern imagery, and now threatens the North's racial and economic status quo. Again, the racial Other—the black man's phallus and the black woman's womb—must be framed within acceptable imagery.

In *Birth of A Nation*, Griffith consolidated the current racial stereotypes and received praise from the Democratic President Woodrow Wilson. *Birth* portrays the educated and not-so-educated black man as a rapist and prone to political graft; he is the source of all criminality in the South.

The film presents an obese maidservant (a white woman in blackface) who protects the white daughter of a liberal politician from the sexual advances of his protégé, an educated mulatto politician. Gus, an unruly black field hand, is another black male who has lust for a white woman. Gus chases the white daughter of a dispossessed southern planter until she escapes by throwing herself from a cliff. In reaction to these black men and those blacks who have taken over the state government, the Klan organizes to protect the South and its women from upstart mulatto politicians and unruly bucks like Gus.

Griffith's catalogue of black types consists of popular images of blacks from the pre-Civil War- and Reconstruction-eras. According to the film, the black community is prone to violence, political corruption, and rape if they are not submissive to whites. Therefore, blacks require such extralegal policing mechanisms as white vigilantes, city-sponsored Rodney King beatings, and state-financed executions. Griffith's narrative presents the black community as the racial "other" who is most threatening when not policed by the Ku Klux Klan.

After World War I, the Ku Klux Klan used the film to rejuvenate the Klan and enlist members in its northern chapters. Similarly, during the 1988 presidential elections, the Republican Party borrowed the Klan's racist strategy to rejuvenate their political party and enlarge its membership. The Republican campaign took Griffith's construction of the oversexed black man and threatened the white American electorate with the image of Willy Horton, a convicted rapist who, upon his early parole from a Maryland prison, raped a white woman. Most criticism leveled at the Republican Party's use of Horton viewed it as a direct attack on the Democrat Party's president-elect Michael Dukakis who, as the Governor of Massachusetts, signed for Willy Horton's early parole. I, however, view the use of Willy Horton as an expressed fear of Jesse Jackson, a major Democrat contender for the presidency in 1988. One must remember that in the film *Birth*, the political prominence and lusty nature of black men codify the sexual and political fears of white patriarchy whose extremist organizations, like the Klan and the Aryan Nation, are no less lethal than an unchecked Simi Valley jury.

Birth's portrayal of the Ku Klux Klan resembles such individual heroes as Rambo and Rocky. The three images—the KKK, Rambo, and Rocky—protect the real and imagined black threats to white patriarchal systems. These images safeguard land and white womanhood. For entertainment purposes, all three animate their narratives with sentimentality and are most popular when the status quo comes to grips with the uncertainty of their position. Nevertheless, racist patriarchal systems continue to employ "real" and imaginary heroes as their agents who use such extralegal forms of suppression as beatings, rapes, bombings, and executions. Thus, even the banality of negotiating a docile behavior, as Mr. Rodney King attempted, will not deter these agents of white patriarchal ordering. The postNegritude response to persistent forms of physical and sociopsychic attacks remains provisional. Still, "to educate (wo)man to be *actional*, preserving in all his (or her) relations . . . (a) respect for the basic values that constitute a human world, is the prime task of him (or her) who, having taken thought, prepares to act."[6] PostNegritude resists the appropriation of reactionary strategies that imitate repressive forms of imaginary narratives as well as "real" systems of extralegal physical abuse.

Recently, American film studios have churned out nostalgic melodramas about the 1960s Civil Rights movement. The films show racial injustices as a solely southern phenomenon. Why is there no cycle of films depicting racism in northern cities like Chicago, Boston, and New York? The history of northern white vigilantes and their murderous raids on black communities in the early 1900s remains a black hole—full of history but seemingly empty of contents. The American popular imagination cannot digest the beating of Rodney King because it did not occur in the South. Equally absurd is America's inability to understand why and how a middle-class suburban community found the Los Angeles police officers not guilty for the beating of King. If these two miscarriages of justice had taken place in the South, however, the explanation would be all too obvious. In the popular mind, the South is the *bête noire* of America's racism. Popular American media conditions audiences to accept racism and its murderous history as a rural southern landscape. In the popular mind, there remains a total ignorance of the North's subtle acquiescence in racial segregation and lynching.

Most of the recent cycle of Civil Rights melodramas, like Alan Parker's *Mississippi Burning* (1988), Bruce Beresford's Atlanta-based *Driving Miss Daisy* (1989), and Richard Pearce's Alabama-situated *A Long Walk Home* (1991), deal with the pre-Civil Rights era. Even Edward Zwick's Civil War epic *Glory* (1989) deals with a classical Civil Rights issue—the integration of an all black regiment into a predominantly white Union Army. The films portray the initial battle for racial integration, a battle whose legal ally is the establishment of federal civil right laws. Independently produced films like Martin Scorsese's *Boxcar Bertha* (1972), Barbara Kopple's *Harlan County U.S.A.* (1976), and John Sayles's *Matewan* (1987) have filmed southern landscapes in which interracial and womanist solidarity coalesces against anti-unionist, racist, and sexist power elites who prefer to see whites, blacks, and women fighting each other on and off the movie screen.

POSTNEGRITUDE AND JULIE DASH'S MAGICAL WOMEN

1991 marked the appearance of Julie Dash's *Daughters of the Dust*. The film presents a nonlinear narrative about an extended family of Gullah women who inhabit an island off the Georgia and South Carolina coast. *Daughters of the Dust* creates a pluralistic understanding of womanism and women's rights. The film uses a nonclassical narrative style that fragments temporal and spatial divisions. Different female narrators tell the story and these narrators, when taken together, reveal a complex understanding of the Peazant family. Previous southern films about blacks feature southern male protagonists as villainous white men and the white northern liberal as the savior of victimized members of the black community. Unlike most of the southern films mentioned earlier, *Daughters of the Dust* is a women-centered film that develops interesting portraits of its female protagonists.

Ibo Landing, one of a hundred of sea islands off the Georgia and South Carolina coast, is the setting of *Daughters of the Dust*. It is 1902 and the Peazants, an extended African American family of Gullah people, prepare for their departure from Ibo Landing. The landing has been the home of the Peazant family for several generations. The eldest Peazant, Nana, is an eighty-eight-year-old matriarch. Nana guards the African religious rituals and cures which West African slaves taught her. The members of the Peazant family are the direct descendants of these West African slaves who lived on Ibo Landing.

The eminent departure of the younger generation of Peazants worries Nana but she rejects their overtures for her to accompany them to the North. She fears that such a move would break her connection with her African ancestors who lay buried on Ibo Landing. Her knowledge of the family's oral history, her medicinal use of the island fauna are daily rituals that she does not want to take to the mainland. Nana believes that a better life is not possible by leaving Ibo landing or accepting Christianity. Nevertheless, the other members of the clan continue their plans as Nana seeks help from the spirits of her dead ancestors.

Throughout the film, their spirits are given life in the voice of Nana who speaks of the Peazant's West African heritage. Nana, the family griot, nurtures her fragmenting family with knowledge of Yoruba religious and medicinal practices. Her narrative instills pride and recounts the Peazant family history. Nana's increasing age has not dulled her memory and spirit. She is a root doctor and spiritual leader who rejects the temptation of modernism and a better life on the mainland. Nana's consciousness supplies the voice-over as it languidly guides the camera through Ibo Landing's luscious vegetation where a family album of white-linen-clad people of yellow, brown, and blue-black complexions live.

There are a few formidable obstacles that place Nana's spirit and, thereby, the well-being of the Peazant family, in flux. The Peazant family's departure from Ibo Landing and Nana means leaving a West African past and its rituals. Many family members view Nana's religious practices as primitive and un-Christian. Viola Peazant wants the family to go North under the protection of Christianity; she wants the family to migrate to the North and leave the Yoruba gods and goddesses and its main priestess Nana. Haagar Peazant echoes Viola's Christian entreaties. Haagar, a woman who married into the Peazant clan, is Nana's most vocal critic. Haagar argues for northern migration because it will improve their lives. Haagar accepts Christianity and ardently criticizes Nana's folk remedies and Yoruba practices. Ignoring the barking of Haagar, Nana converses with her deceased elders and asks them to guide the departing Peazant members; before their departure, she instills in every Peazant a reverence for their Yoruba past which she says will guide them on their great migration to the North.

Next, Nana calls on Yoruba spirits to safeguard her granddaughter Eula's marriage with Eli, a man who believes that his wife is pregnant with the child of a white rapist.

Throughout the film, white people are visually absent yet their ominous off-screen presence cannot be denied. For example, Eli fears that a white man raped his wife; he has a burgeoning interest in the antilynching movement on the mainland. And Yellow Mary, another Peazant woman, tells of how white men abused her body. These elements all provide *Daughters* with a sort of enduring critique of racism. The film, however, does not allow racism to destroy the spirituality of the Peazant women and their family even though Eli leaves his pregnant wife Eula and joins the antilynching campaign. Ibo land remains sacred ground inhabited by Nana, Yellow Mary, Haagar's daughter, and Eula and her newborn daughter. Unlike the Peazant family who leaves Ibo Landing, Nana's black matriarchal community includes women who have been sexually abused and one woman who returned to the island after experiencing life on the mainland. In a voice-over narration, the daughter of Eula brings the film to its end as most of the Peazant clan board a boat for the mainland.

Daughters of the Dust resists beliefs, sociocultural customs, and newfangled ideas that inhibit individual growth. Modernism and Christianity have been accepted by many of the Peazants but their acceptance of the new works against Nana's celebration of African rituals. Nana Peazant creates spiritual and loving places for a new generation to ponder over and work to rebuild.

POSTNEGRITUDE ERUPTIONS:
ANITA HILL AND CLARENCE THOMAS

An editorial in *The Nation* asserts that Anita Hill's "charge of sexual harassment is simply another reminder of the inextricable relationship of personal and public life." I would like to pursue a narrower focus on the Hill and Thomas fiasco. The American public has certainly discovered that there are political divisions within the African American community. Furthermore, even though the media has constructed or permitted the construction of a high-tech lynching of both of these black individuals, the black female embodied in Professor Hill is the one who remains the lynched victim. Hill, not Thomas, is the victim, as is the community of women's rights advocates who must witness this Ralph Ellison-like Battle Royal between two members of the highly educated and politically conservative African American middle class. W.E.B. DuBois refers to this group of black achievers as the "Talented Tenth" of the black community. What has become of this promising group and those interracial progressives who led the Civil Rights and Women's Movements of the fifties, sixties and seventies? Unfortunately, they must observe the talking heads of the lily-white male senators framed on the television screen. This is a carnival of conservative disgust in a not-so-democratic American melodrama. The omnipotent have manned the cameras to psychologically strip search and visually lynch blacks. In the name of Justice for Mr. Thomas and/or Professor Hill, they have spun the wheel of sexual harassment. With television ratings at their lowest, they introduce Judge Thomas's Night Court that becomes a three-day mini-series aired on national and public television. Frantz Fanon provides a psychoanalytical language to explain the Hill and Thomas high-tech lynching staged by lily-white impresarios of the Democratic and Republican parties. He argues,

> If one wants to understand the racial situation psycho-analytically, not from a universal viewpoint but as it is experienced by individual consciousnesses, considerable importance must be given to sexual phenomena. In the case of the Jew, one thinks of money and its cognates. In that of the Negro, one thinks of sex.[7]

Can supporters of Anita Hill ignore the all-too-familiar racist undertones of "Long Dong Silver." Perhaps Robert Mapplethorpe's photograph "Man in Polyester Suit"[8] anticipates the media's portrait of Judge Thomas. When the Thomasites surmise that Anita Hill is a scorned woman and has delusions, they articulate the essence of patriarchal wisdom gone amuck. What is being constructed in the most paternal and benign manner are racist and misogynist myths. Unfortunately, these myths are generated by and for conservative and, seemingly, liberal causes, which include the maintenance of a two-party political system circumscribed by the simulacra of opposition discourses uttered by senators from the Republican and Democratic Parties.

Roland Barthes writes,

> The petit-bourgeois is a man unable to imagine the Other. If he comes face to face with him, he blinds himself, ignores and denies him, or else transforms him into himself. In the petit-bourgeois universe, all the experiences of confrontation are reverberating, any otherness is reduced to sameness. The spectacle or the tribunal, which are both places where the Other threatens to appear in full view, become mirrors. This is because the Other is a scandal which threatens his essence. . . . Justice is a weighing operation and . . . scales can only weigh like against like.[9]

The Hill/Thomas hearings involve two racial Others and one gendered Other. Some might criticize the manner in which the news media constructs Professor Hill because the articles emphasize her gender while they tend to underestimate the cultural differences between African American and Anglo-American women. I do not agree with these criticisms because they overemphasize race-specific cultural difference which ignores the hegemony of sexism and white-collar professionalism. To argue for such a race-based understanding of sexual harassment in the Hill-Thomas affair oversimplifies the work experiences of African American professional women. This begs one to reconsider and then dismiss criteria based solely on racial experience, because it cannot explain the survival strategies of black professional women such as Anita Hill. Any interpretation of Anita Hill's success within a male-centered and racist system would not prioritize racial solidarity. Such a priority would involve ignoring the intraracial rift between two African Americans, Professor Anita Hill and Judge Clarence Thomas.

The erasures of cultural and gender differences are best described by Barthes who explains how

> the Other is revealed as irreducible: not because of a sudden scruple, but because common sense rebels: a man does not have a white skin, but a black one, another drinks pear juice,

not Pernod. How can one assimilate the Negro, the Russian?
. . . For, even if he is unable to experience the Other himself,
the bourgeois can at least imagine the place where he fits in.[10]

Judge Thomas becomes "Long Dong Silver" or Mapplethorpe's "Man
in the Polyester Suit" while Professor Hill is the hysterical black woman
or the black bitch. According to Barthes,

> this is what is known as liberalism, which is a sort of intellec-
> tual equilibrium based on recognized places. The petit-
> bourgeois class is not liberal (it produces Fascism, whereas
> the bourgeoisie uses it): it follows the same route as the
> bourgeoisie, but lags behind.[11]

In this scenario, Professor Anita Hill occupies an extreme instance of
the marginal black Other. For it is Hill, not Thomas, whose lynching is
brought on by the fact of her gender and her race. Hill's lynching benefits the political agendas of petit-bourgeois Republicans who construct
such fascism as The Gulf War, the Invasion of Panama, the nightmare
of a Willie Horton with flashbacks of David Duke, and the discourse of
"the delusionary black woman."

In keeping with my position that the Gulf War is fascist, I am
here asserting a postNegritude challenge to the dominant rationale
for the war. My argument is that the Gulf War was a technologically
sanitized colonial war to safeguard multinational oil interests—the
same multinational interests that recently permitted the Nigerian
junta to imprison and then hang the Nigerian-Ogoni writer Ken Saro-
Wiwa and several other members of the Ogoni tribe. The Gulf War
and the assassination of Saro-Wiwa are fascist acts because such
deaths are the indirect effects of multinational oil companies, like
Shell Oil, whose unconscionable economic controls suppress the opposition through terror and censorship. In protecting Saudi Arabia
and the Gulf oil fields, the United States government's deployment of
smart bombs and Shell Oil's present despoliation of Nigeria's
Ogoniland have surely affected the world ecosystem in similar ways.
In turn, these ecological and moral atrocities are similar to the ecological and moral consequences of the use of atomic warfare against
Japan. Yes, the smart bomb and the atomic bomb differ in the degree
of their lethal effects, but they do not much differ in the systemically
amoral and economic reasoning that lies behind them.

Unfortunately, rank-and-file Democrats permit the circulation of such fascist productions in the name of liberalism and the spectacle of "First Amendment Rights" equilibrium. In echoing Barthes' discussion of the Other, W. Lawrence Hogue observes,

> The exclusion of the Afro-American has more to do with the discursive formation that defines whites' definition of reality (the media) than it has to do with intentional, motivated racism. But the images and myths invested in the Afro-American become integral practices within the dominant ideological apparatus. They become a part of the myth of an American consensus.[12]

SPIKE LEE'S *MALCOLM X*: WHOSE X IS IT?

In the sixties, few people could imagine that by the nineties, interest in Malcolm X would again dominate American popular culture in such an unthreatening way. The legend of Malcolm X has been reinvented. His emblematic presence shares a decade with two of the most disgusting displays of racism and sexism on our most sacred international altar—the television. I am here referring to the Rodney King beating and the Anita Hill-Clarence Thomas case and their lily-white and very male lynch mobs. Both instances reflect the ongoing struggle with residual forms of racial and sexual oppression. The postNegritude struggle views race, gender, sexuality, and class as interconnected battles without national borders. American television programs and films are not confined to an American constituency. American media resemble the smart bombs that search for Iraqi military targets and kill innocent civilians who are in their path. Smart bombs poison the ecosystem while media bombs poison the psycho-system. Neither of the two bombs discerns civilian subjects from military objects nor recognizes the tension between hyphenated nationalists and those exiled beings who are in constant unfolding.

Thus, one can be at a baptism in southwestern France and yet be questioned regarding the Simi Valley jury who found the Los Angeles police officers not guilty of their brutal beating of the African American motorist, Rodney King. One can also be asked about the appropriateness of Clarence Thomas as a Supreme Court Justice.

Both Alex Haley's *The Autobiography of Malcolm X* and Lee's film document the life of one of America's most militant black nationalist leaders. Presently, the film, the autobiography, and the other Malcolm X popular icons, attract a racially and politically mixed audience. Together, these images revive African American interest in Islam, nationalism, conspiracy theories, protest strategies, and the increasing importance of *local* and *international* liberation struggles.

Lee's creative genius lies in his ability to construct Malcolm for three very different groups: first, his college-educated and racially mixed film audience who flock to see whatever is his most recent film; second, the black audience in search of films by black filmmakers; and lastly and most importantly, his film distributor, the multinational media conglomerate Time-Warner Inc. These three constituencies determine how Lee *frames* Malcolm for the multicultural nineties and its discontents.

Lee's camera caresses his audience with a spectacle of a streetwise Malcolm Little. In an intimate scene between Malcolm and his white girlfriend Sophia, Lee has Malcolm tell Sophia to kiss his foot. Lee's depiction of this interracial affair is more imagined than real. Malcolm was not as critical of this form of intimacy. When Malcolm X was asked, "Are you against love between a white person and a black person?" he replied, "how can anyone be against love? Whoever a person wants to love that's their business—that's like their religion."[13] Lee negates this image of Malcolm and presents his version of Malcolm who speaks with a Spike Lee tongue. In this *re*-visioned Malcolm, Lee projects his personal disgust for his white stepmother.

For the most part, he portrays Betty Shabazz as an obedient and complacent woman. In so doing, Lee obscures the strong-willed, nursing-school trained woman who, on several occasions, took her children and left a self-absorbed Malcolm X. This omission permits Lee to focus on the legend; but it also indicates how Lee's masculinist sentiments portray women in this film. Lee's depiction of Malcolm, Sophia, and Betty does not square with the documentary artifacts that constitute another slippery but more factual image of Malcolm.

The less fictional regimes of truth resist Lee's narrow focus on a young and politically naive Malcolm. Alex Haley's *The Autobiography of Malcolm X*, Malcolm's published speeches, and his television interviews resist Lee's canted frames. Admittedly most, if not all, histories

Figure 1. Gangster Boss West Indian Archie (Delroy Lindo) threatens his protégé, Malcolm Little (Denzel Washington). Photo by David Lee/Warner Bros.

contain certain amounts of questionable claims. Lee's film, however, is more fiction than real, and, unfortunately, more accessible than the other regimes of truth. Lee's film will determine how most moviegoers come to "know" Malcolm Little, Malcolm X, and El-Hadjj Malik El-Shabazz. This is especially true when many audience members have not, and will not, refer to such extrafilmic documents as his speeches, taped television interviews, and the sociopolitical world that surrounded him.

Malcolm's face and the enigmatic X have become an advertisement for black nationalist political sentiment. Malcolm's emblematic face and his mark of excellence illustrate the inherent contradictions in Malcolm's protean life which Lee frames in medium close-ups. Lee's close-ups, however, never reveal why Malcolm's entrance into political activism angered the Nation of Islam's conservative leadership; and his camera refuses to dramatize the growing hostility between Malcolm and certain ministers in the Nation of Islam. The film never reveals how certain Nation of Islam ministers attempted to weaken Malcolm's influence over Black Muslims, black nationalists, and the younger members in the civil rights movement. Because Lee avoids treating controversial issues within the Nation of Islam, he inadvertently produces a monolithic image of the Nation and the various types of black nationalist thought.

The film explains Malcolm's rejection of the teachings of Elijah Muhammad as a reaction to his fathering several illegitimate children. Yes, one can reject his immoral actions but why extend this rejection to the Honorable Elijah Muhammad's teachings? Consequently, Lee presents Malcolm's political vision as concurring with that of Elijah Muhammad and the present Nation of Islam. Ironically, the figure of Minister Louis Farrakhan is absent from any part of the film. His absence is quite telling, since he was one of Malcolm's protégés, and later became one of his severest critics. Clayborne Carson reports that

> Soon after his return to the United States, Malcolm's house was firebombed. He attributed the act to his enemies in the Nation of Islam. While the identity of the arsonist was never determined, Malcolm's public criticisms of Elijah Muhammad had unquestionably made him a target for Muslim zealots. During December, Fruit of Islam Captain Raymond Sharrieff had sent an open telegram to Malcolm officially warning him that 'the Nation of Islam shall no longer tolerate your scandalizing the name of our leader and teacher, the Honorable Elijah Muhammad. ... Minister Louis X (later Louis Farrakkan), once Malcolm's protege, also attacked his former friend in strong terms.[14]

As I mentioned earlier, Lee takes artistic license when he portrays Malcolm's interracial affair with Sophia and denies an empowered image of Malcolm's wife Betty Shabazz. Paradoxically, Lee's artistic license also permits him to defer any suggestion that Minister Louis Farrakkhan was one of the Muslims who threatened Malcolm's life. The film denigrates transracial unions, obscures Betty Shabazz's self-determination, and hides the political battle Malcolm waged against certain ministers in the Nation of Islam. In the areas of race, gender, and international politics, the film projects an unthreatening image to both white and black audiences who honor such additions and omissions. It is incumbent upon those who affirm a transracial and transgendered identity to resist Lee's frame, just as Malcolm resisted the apolitical stance of the Honorable Elijah Muhammad.

Figure 2. Elijah Muhammad (Al Freeman Jr.), the spiritual leader of the Nation of Islam, confers with his spokesman, Malcolm X (Denzel Washington).

Instead of revealing the internal disagreements that led Malcolm to establish the Organization of African American Unity, Lee's camera ponderously lingers on Malcolm's threats of black retaliatory violence. It is true that Malcolm's emphatic posturing and rhetorical threats signaled his difference from Dr. King's strategy of passive resistance. It is also true that Malcolm attracted a new generation of black activists, such as the Black Panthers and the more radical members of the Student Nonviolent Coordinating Committee (SNCC). This new generation had grown tired of nonviolent tactics. In stressing the importance of violence and emphatic posturing, Lee's film exaggerates the meaning of Malcolm's "By Any Means Necessary," and uncritically proposes the use of indiscriminate violence of the Reginald Denny kind.

Black films that propose the indiscriminate use of violence are detrimental to the community. In hindsight, it was suicidal when a generation of young black men openly confronted the police during the sixties. In the nineties, when black-on-black crime is killing off the next generation of potential black leaders, it is *still* suicidal to overtly celebrate and threaten police with violence.

Returning to the expression "by any means necessary," the phrase has more resonance when it is used to describe an anticolonial struggle waged by a psychologically colonized people. Therein, it means to pursue an education while maintaining a sense of self-respect and self-determination. However, if one encounters physical aggression, and obstacles are placed in the path to these goals, then one must obtain them "by any means necessary." Not only does this understanding require that one discern the difference between various forms of violence, it confirms the traditional trajectory in which African American slaves secured their physical and psychological liberation.

Lastly, the film shows Malcolm as he meets with an international, poly-racial community during his visit to Mecca. Lee's camera, however, misses an opportunity to present how and why Malcolm reappraises the "white man." Considering the film's length, Lee portrays Malcolm's reappraisal of white people in an all-too-easy manner. Additionally, Malcolm's conversion to a transracial Islam seems premature, because Lee maintains an image of Malcolm as denying the feasibility of a transracial struggle against racism and colonialism. True, there are similar evasions in Haley's *The Autobiography of Malcolm X*, but a film of such epic length should not replicate the errors of its literary source.

The film concludes by simple-mindedly linking Malcolm X to Nelson Mandela. This intellectual montage fails to connect the two contrasting liberation philosophies of these men. Blackness is not so simple and liberation struggles are not all the same, regardless of their similar black hue and racist enemies. Lee ignores the vast difference between black separatism and democratic socialism that Malcolm X and Nelson Mandela espouse, respectively. There needs to be some explanation for Malcolm's reappraisal of the white man, and, thereby, the film would show that Malcolm no longer practiced a racialist form of black nationalism. Lee's use of montage editing wrongly suggests that Malcolm X and Nelson Mandela share a similar philosophical trajectory. This closure contradicts the film's construction of Malcolm as an advocate of a separatist type of black nationalism. Contrary to Malcolm's separatist platform, Nelson Mandela works with an interracial organization and opposes the politics of racial separatism as practiced in South Africa.

Similarly, Lee's Rodney King-American Flag montage expresses the unforgettable history of racial lynching. Again, the abused body of Rodney King should not be separated from his thoughtful words in

Figure 3. Shorty (Spike Lee) is held at gunpoint by New York City's finest. Photo by David Lee/Warner Bros.

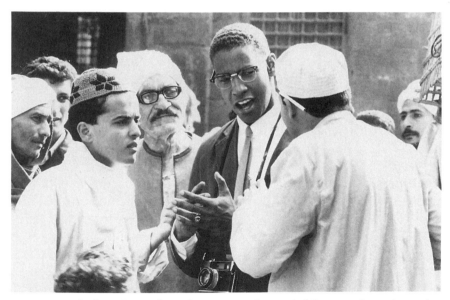

Figure 4. Malcolm X (Denzel Washington) confers with fellow Moslems during his pilgrimmage to Mecca.

reaction to the beating. As it stands, the film provides little evidence of the complex nature of racism; even though Lee introduces his film with the videotaped beating of Rodney King, he somehow forgets that white Reginald Denny was also brutally beaten by racists.

The film unwittingly links Malcolm X to Nelson Mandela, Rodney King, and nameless black school children. This type of "we are the world" closure becomes a sort of currency of victimization, which is tendered but never fully explained.

Overall then, the film accurately portrays Malcolm X lecturing on the importance of self-respect, economic self-determination, and the sociophysical liberation of Black people. Unfortunately, Lee's film elides Malcolm's argument with the apolitical philosophy of the Nation of Islam, and it avoids presenting Malcolm's ideological battles with the reactionary members of the Nation. Besides this omission, and underlining Lee's aim to avoid a Salman Rushdie-like death threat, Louis Farrakkhan is totally absent from the film, though he played an important role in condemning Malcolm. Lee emphasizes the early life of Malcolm in order to stress "by any means necessary" violence and racial and sexual chauvinism; therein Lee buries Malcolm's critique of neocolonialism in Southeast Asia, Africa, and the Caribbean; and he overlooks Betty Shabazz's resistance to her husband's short-sighted political vision. Undoubtedly, Lee's film charms an interracial audience who, like Malcolm, views the world in manichean terms and, thereby, ignores that Rodney King and Reginald Denny are equal victims of racism.

Lee's *Malcolm X* celebrates a nostalgic, sociopsychical terrain, inhabited by racially fixed black and white male anatomics. The X-brand marks the in-between and slippery currency of popular American racial sentiment. Each visually excised portrait of Malcolm Little, Detroit Red, Malcolm X, and El-Hajj Malik El-Shabazz, is separated by a postmodern frontier of "by-any-means-necessary" consumerism. Near the consumer lies discontented spaces in which struggles are waged rather than bought. The "in-gods-we-trust" currencies are no longer negotiable at their previous rate. A womanist politics intervenes at the borders of Lee's frame and walks among the transgendered, transracial, transsexual orientations in fluid social motion and social momentum.[15] Within this postNegritude space the Blackness of Rodney King and the Whiteness of Reginald Denny become human problems with possible solutions.

Figure 5. Angie Tucci (Annabella Sciorra). Photo by David Lee.

Figure 6. Flipper Purify (Wesley Snipes). Photo by David Lee.

SPIKE LEE'S *JUNGLE FEVER:* RACE, SEX, AND THE IN-BETWEENS

My assessment of African American cultural studies describes the dissolution of racial dualism as a paradigm for explaining the totality of black experiences. In some instances, race is an arbitrary term which requires contextualization and the consideration of other issues. For example, South Africa's legal distinction between "Coloreds" and "Blacks," or Brazil's copious list of terms to describe the complexion of its Afro-Brazilian citizens, or the United States notion that one drop of African blood places the person in a black category, these are examples of the arbitrary nature of race. Race, therefore, is a social construction rather than a biological given.

When black cultural critics speak of this racial arbitrariness and discuss issues of class, gender, and sexual orientation, they describe black culture within the postNegritude. This moment evokes free zones of discourse in which extraracial minority discourses are uttered.

> Minority discourse implies that it is the perpetual return of theory to the concrete givens of domination, rather that the separation of culture as a discrete sphere, that militates against the reification of any dominated group's experience as in some sense "privileged." Just as domination works by con-

stant adjustment, so the strategies of the dominated must remain fluid in their objects as in their solidarities.[16]

Certain black-directed films have militated against the reification of the
dominated black protagonist's experience as one which privileges the
racial over other issues. In discussing this, I will focus my attentions on
Jungle Fever's dramatization of interracial intimacy on two narrative
levels—the Negritude and the postNegritude.

Spike Lee's fifth film, *Jungle Fever* (1991), depicts interracial love,
lust, and hate between the Italian American residents of the Brooklyn
neighborhood of Bensonhurst and the African American residents of
the New York City neighborhood of Harlem.

In *Jungle Fever*, Lee presents two different types of interracial
sexual intimacy. One of the film's representations of love meanders in a
serpent-like fashion through the African American loins of Flipper
Purify to the Italian American heart of Angie Tucci, Flipper's temporary secretary. The other portrait, a postNegritude vision, concerns
Paulie Carbone, an Italian American and Orin Goode, an African
American woman.

The film's title and much of the dialogue would have us believe
that both Flipper's and Angie's motivations are determined by "jungle
fever," which describes a sensual adventure through the blackest and
whitest terrains of sexuality in its most physical and psychological manifestations. In this study I argue, however, that the film subtly ruptures
the jungle-fever discourse that interracial intimacy is doomed to failure.
The difference between Angie and Flipper is inscribed in their class,
their marital status, and their race. The conventions that organize class,
marriage, and race deny Angie and Flipper success in their romance.
The film does not totally reject all forms of interracial intimacy.

The Angie-Flipper love affair challenges three social taboos that
determine the failure of their relationship. First, their love affair violates
a social taboo against interracial sexual intimacy; second, it transgresses
both religious and social conventions against adultery; and third, their
union defies the unwritten law of black bourgeois success which denies
lasting interracial love affairs with the white lower classes. I will now
discuss how each of these transgressions affects the development of the
film's main narrative level.

Flipper is husband to Drew, a mulatto, and he is father to Ming, a
prepubescent girl. Flipper, Drew, and Ming represent the conventional

Figure 7. Ming Purify (Veronica Timbers), Drew Purify (Lonette McKee), and Flipper Purify (Wesley Snipes). Photo courtesy BFI Stills, Posters and Designs.

black middle-class family. Flipper is a successful architect and Drew is a buyer for Bloomingdales, an upscale Manhattan clothing store. The Purify family lives in a Harlem brownstone apartment that is furnished with all the electronic gadgets of life in the nineties.

Flipper's temporary secretary Angie Tucci has a family situation far different from that of the Purify nuclear family. Angie lives in a Brooklyn bungalow located in the infamous community of Bensonhurst. She lives with her widowed father and two brothers for whom she cooks after she has returned from her secretarial job. The film portrays the Tucci men as distinct members of the Italian American working class. The film establishes their ethnicity in their language, their spaghetti dinner, and their Catholicism. Angie belongs to an Italian American working-class family but desires something that her family, her Bensonhurst neighbors, her Catholic upbringing, and her boyfriend Paulie has neither given her nor permitted her to experience. Angie's life lacks a sensual romantic adventure. This deficiency in her sexual life leads her into an amorous adventure with a married black man. Angie's Italian American family, her Bensonhurst community, her Catholic upbringing, and even her sensitive boyfriend cannot and would not offer her such a romantic choice.

In the film's first scene, we visually witness Ming listening to the ecstatic screams of Drew as Flipper makes love to her. This scene informs us that sex with Flipper is gratifying and even his young daughter knows of its pleasure. Flipper, however, is not satisfied with making love to Drew and develops an adulterous relationship with Angie. On the second day of Angie's job as Flipper's temporary secretary, they work into the evening, eat Chinese food, exchange knowing glances, and begin their sensual mixing of the races. Neither their parents, nor Flipper's wife and Angie's boyfriend, nor their best friends, nor their racial and ethnic communities condone sexual intercourse between the races or sex between married men and single women.

Cyrus, a black boyhood friend of Flipper, describes Flipper and Angie's attraction as a case of jungle fever. After Flipper indulges his fever, he severs his relationship with Angie to whom he repeats Cyrus's jungle-fever analysis. Flipper's change results from at least three social pressures he is faced with: (1) the unwarranted attack by the police because he was with a white woman; (2) his adultery leading to alienation from his wife and daughter; and (3) Angie's limited education and lower class status. Angie cannot replace his wife Drew who helps Flipper attain his middle-class socioeconomic status. Like a martyr, Angie accepts rejection by her clan and resists Flipper's description of their love as one of racial lust. The narrative elements that structure romance want us to believe that Angie sincerely loves Flipper. And because of her love for Flipper, she breaks off her relationship with her high-school boyfriend Paulie. Angie's devotion is romantically constructed.

Flipper's velvety blackness, his middle-class status and his professional education might have attracted Angie. It is, however, Angie's northern, Italian, marble whiteness that evokes the white patriarchal discourse on the primitive lust between the races. The racist discourse of the phallic jungle views Flipper's black vein as giving demonic value to Angie's pure northern marble. The same discourse permits Flipper's darkness to render Drew, his mulatto wife, blacker than her near-white complexion indicates. Flipper's motivation reflects the primitive and racist discourse which is shared by Angie's father. Consequently, he beats Angie after learning about her black boyfriend Flipper. Her father has undergone an emasculation. The Angie-Flipper relationship cannot escape the determinism of white patriarchal authority, which also

Figure 8a. Widower Mike Tucci (Frank Vincent) eats dinner with his children Charlie (David Dundara), Angie (Annabella Sciorra), and James (Michael Imperioli). Photo by David Lee.

Figure 8b. Flipper's father, the Good Reverend Doctor (Ossie Davis), argues with Flipper's mother, Lucinda (Ruby Dee), and Flipper and his girlfriend, Angie, look on. Photo by David Lee.

surfaces in the white police officers, who stop the two lovers and place a gun to the head of Flipper. It is a struggle over who controls the female body, a struggle between men who deny the self-determination of one woman. In reality, Angie determines when and where these men

Figure 9. Flipper and Angie become romantically intertwined on a polished wooden floor. Photo by David Lee.

enter to abuse her in their own very malevolent ways: one as a lover, another as a weak father, and the two police officers who serve and protect the components of white patriarchy—including Catholic girls, like Angie, who have left their church and homes to roam the wild urban prairies of multicultural America.

One question haunts the racist discourse of the phallic jungle: If there wasn't a near-white Drew would there be a too-white Angie? This concern ignores the always existing dialogue between the racist discourse of the phallic jungle and those peripheral discourses that make Lee's film a complex statement on interracial intimacy.

Figure 10. Flipper and Angie embrace in a pub(l)ic space. Photo courtesy BFI Stills, Posters and Designs.

Figure 11. A police officer points a gun to Flipper's head after having witnessed Flipper's playful romp with Angie, his white Italian American girlfriend. Photo courtesy BFI Stills, Posters and Designs.

Angie's initial attraction to Flipper is provoked by a multitude of urges that do not deny Flipper's blackness, but do not limit his blackness to fictions about black and white sexuality. Flipper is psychologically defeated when he accepts the jungle-fever myth uttered by black and white characters and enforced by their social institutions. He limits his identity to a phallic racialist vision that begins and ends flaccid between his loins. The jungle-fever analysis enlivens a death dance with sexual myths that condemn Flipper, Drew, and Angie.

According to African American common wisdom, the Flipper and Angie love affair fails because it is against middle-class morality, class consciousness, and racial conventions. Flipper's marriage, his race, and his middle-class aspirations destroy any chance of a prolonged union with Angie. Flipper has too much to lose and only love to gain. And as the refrain goes, "What does love have to do with it?" Their affair cannot be sustained for reasons that exceed those based on racial factors. His middle-class aspirations do not permit him to have a working-class woman as a mate, any more than his adulterous act can be condoned by his equally middle-class professional wife. The middle-class narrative structure requires that adultery be punished. Thus, the narrative demands the termination of the Angie-Flipper relationship.

The film *Jungle Fever* also presents the beginnings of an interracial romance between Paulie Carbone and Orin Goode. With the introduction of the Orin-Paulie friendship, Spike Lee subtly diverts attention away from a negative portrayal of interracial love to challenge the arguments against it. Unlike the interracial affair of Flipper and Angie that transgresses America's marital, class, and racial conventions, the Paulie and Orin relationship only challenges racial conventions. Orin Goode, a black college student, frequents Paulie's Bensonhurst candy store where she daily buys a newspaper and encourages Paulie to attend college. When she leaves, the young, white neighborhood toughs express how much they would like to have sex with Orin. Ironically, the neighborhood's toughs echo the white patriarchal discourse and express their primordial fear of black male sexuality, while they fervently boast of their lust for a black woman.

None of these young white men want to publicly acknowledge their attraction through the conventional channels of dating or marriage. There are no policemen to point their guns. There are no Italian American fathers to beat these young men senseless for entertaining a forbidden thought. These neighborhood men are their own policing force who beat Paulie when he acts upon his desires in a very human way.

Figure 12. Paulie Carbone (John Turturro) oversees his father's candy store and tries to humanize the Italian American men who congregate in it. Photo courtesy BFI Stills, Posters and Designs.

Unlike their African and Italian American peers, Paulie, Angie, and Orin venture into an unknown territory that borders the marginal worlds of both the African and Italian American subcultures and deny the sexual myths which stagnate these worlds. Different from the Angie-Flipper border crossing, Paulie survives the physical and psychological attacks that his father and the young Italian American toughs direct at both his mind and body. He triumphantly strides toward Orin's apartment, an open racial and ethnic space in which the postNegritude intersects with free zones of multiple identities.

Jungle Fever concludes with a black middle-class closure that absolves Flipper for his transgressions against family, race, and class unity. The film provides a provisional space for such marginal visionaries as Paulie, Orin, and Angie who have not abandoned the possibility of interracial love. On the border of this space, the cowards like Flipper and the young Italian American toughs stand for a dying racialist paradigm. The two portrayals of interracial intimacy provide *Jungle Fever* with a dialectic that disrupts any attempt to interpret the film as a criticism of

Figure 13. Paulie Carbone (John Turturro) arrives for his first date with Orin Goode (Tyra Ferrell). Photo courtesy BFI Stills, Posters and Designs.

all interracial unions. The film condemns the adulterous affair of Flipper and Angie while it portrays, in a minor chord, the Paulie and Orin relationship as resisting racist ways of thinking which destroyed Angie's romantic advances and catalyzed Flipper's jungle fever.

Spike Lee creates a primitive adventure, a transgressive sexual quest that disturbs family, ethnic, and racial solidarity. *Jungle Fever* is one of Lee's best films because of its complex image of the shared racism of both African and Italian Americans. The film delineates how certain forms of identity interrogate and dismiss racial hierarchies as exemplified in Paulie's sincere attraction to Orin and Angie's romantic attraction to Flipper. Lee's two portrayals of interracial love permit a multiplicity of reconstituted racial, moral, and social others who usually are silenced in mainstream films dealing with interracial intimacy between black and white Americans.

Central to the analysis of the films *Daughters of the Dust, Malcolm X,* and *Jungle Fever,* and the PBS television mini-series "The Anita Hill and Clarence Thomas Affair," is where one locates a postNegritude negotiation between dominant forms of Blackness (read Negritude) and

Figure 14. The two faces of Spike Lee, as Flipper's best friend, Cyrus, and as the protean director and writer of *Jungle Fever*. Photo by David Lee.

the marginal black identities that interrogate and dismiss ethnic, racial, gender, and sexual hierarchies. These marginal interventions into static and monolithic ideas permit the possibility of variance in the constitution of a black diasporic identity that is free to recognize its African and European roots.

In the next chapter, I discuss three representative types of Negritude writing by two African Americans and one Ghanaian during the sixties heyday of the black arts movement. This period of black creativity limited the dramatization of black subjectivity as a struggle between black and white. I have selected John A. Williams's novel *The Man Who Cried I Am* (1967), Ayi Kwei Armah's novel *Fragments* (1969), Adrienne Kennedy's play *The Funnyhouse of a Negro* (1964), and Bob Kaufman's Beat-era poetry to illustrate how four black writers portray their black hero(ine) as mentally crushed by the demands of a masculinist and, sometimes, Afrocentric Negritude project. In Kaufman's poems, the reader finds America as the spiritually crushed heroine.

3

BLACK MASCULINITY
OF THE NEGRITUDE

As the preceding chapter indicates, the fragmentation of monolithic forms of Negritude results in an inclusive form of
Negritude. This form embraces marginal identities that blacks
may share with nonblacks.[1] I call this inclusive form of black subjectivity "postNegritude." This chapter analyzes a few representative examples of 1960s literature that foreshadow the conflicts which would
arise between dominant (Negritude) and marginal (postNegritude)
forms of black identity. Of concern is how this literature depicts the
ideological conflicts that emerge when black subjects resist patriarchy,
racism, and other forms of discrimination. Additionally, the survey
shows how each example dramatizes the contemporary debate over the
constitution of black cultural identity when *race* is no longer (and never
truly was) the sole criterion for defining the black experience.

IN THE SHADOW OF THE BLACK ARTS MOVEMENT

Black writers, like black filmmakers and photographers, have always
participated in the ideological battles over monolithic and multiple
forms of black identity. In its discussion of the postNegritude, the preceding chapter includes black literary works which precede the appearance of the mid-1960s Black Arts movement. This section discusses and
analyzes how selected literary works and the characters in these works

portray multiple and ever-changing black Others as they embrace, sometimes reluctantly and dolefully, a transgendered feminism, a transracial international consciousness, and, when the writer permits, an open-ended sexuality.

I borrow the explanation of Simon Mpondo to describe "the obsessions of the [Negritude] writers" and to provide a literary context to postNegritude. As I have earlier stated, postNegritude has actional characteristics that revise, through negotiation, definitions of Negritude to encompass formerly marginal black others. In describing the ideological work of Negritude writers, Mpondo says,

> They directed their efforts toward fighting smug Caucasians who held them in bondage, reforming institutions which crippled them physically and psychologically, and cultivating artistic expression for whatever benefit they could reap from it. Such efforts were sustained over the years . . . by the assumption that, in each parcel of his life . . . a Negro-African should conform as nearly as possible to norms and standards conceived as immutable and identical for one and all Negroes the world over.[2]

Mpondo states that this mode of literary production created a dominant tendency among these writers. Negritude writers, according to Mpondo, produced "the simplification and homogenization of African intellectual and social life." He goes on to argue that these writers, "succeeded so well in fabricating a Negro collective consciousness that up to today, in Africa, dissent of any sort—especially political and ideological—is seen as an anti-Negro attack which calls for massive retaliation."[3] Even though Mpondo's criticism appears in 1971 and describes a black African literary experience, his general analysis of the weaknesses of Negritude mirrors Frantz Fanon's argument that "the collective unconscious, without having to fall back on the genes, is purely and simply, the sum of prejudices, myths, collective attitudes of a given group. . . . the collective unconscious is cultural, which means acquired."[4] Both statements are relevant to a postNegritude construction of black identity and culture. This more fluid idea of blackness escapes the dogmatic, dehumanizing, and racist genetic propositions which certain blacks and whites circulate for different political reasons. A postNegritude actional remedy reformulates black cultural identity as free from sexual, racial, and religious bigotry.

In *The Order of Things*, Michel Foucault writes "modern thought is advancing towards that region where man's Other must become the Same as himself."[5] Thus, a literary postNegritude is that transitional stage when a significant number of black writers question "the assumption that, in each parcel of . . . [black] life . . . a Negro-African should conform as nearly as possible to norms and standards conceived as immutable and identical for one and all Negroes the world over."[6] In borrowing Houston A. Baker's description of "the deformation of mastery," I describe the difference between black literature that invokes patriarchal conventions and a postNegritude literature that unabashedly rejects such conventions and norms. Baker explains this difference:

> The mastery of [Negritude] form conceals, disguises, floats like a trickster butterfly in order to sting like a bee. The deformation of mastery, by contrast, is Morris Day singing "Jungle Love," advertising, with certainty, his unabashed badness—which is not always conjoined with violence. Deformation [or the postNegritude] is go(uer)rilla action in the face of acknowledged adversaries.[7]

If one considers the different ideological purposes of Negritude and postNegritude writing, one discovers an intertextual dialogue between types of black writing. This intertextuality presents us with one of the many heterogeneous qualities of black literature which works against the Negritude assumption "that, in each parcel of . . . [black] life . . . a Negro-African should conform as nearly as possible to norms and standards conceived as immutable and identical for one and all Negroes the world over."

Henry Louis Gates Jr. describes the intertextuality as "motivated Signifyin(g) in which the text Signifies upon other black texts."[8] In considering the different tactics of Negritude and postNegritude literature, "motivated Signifyin(g)" describes the discursive act exchanged between Negritude and postNegritude writing. "Other black texts" consist of the marginal group of black voices within any single literary (con)text as well as in the institutions that reproduce the order of Negritude simulacra (here, Negritude simulacra refers to monolithic or biologic images of blackness) in literature and the other arts. The black marginal voice may be a timid cry from any, seemingly, "unimportant" character, artist, or audience.

The group of texts that I will discuss consist of four 1960s works: John A. Williams's novel *The Man Who Cried I Am* (1967), Ayi Kwei Armah's novel *Fragments* (1969), Adrienne Kennedy's play *Funnyhouse of a Negro* (1964), and selections from Bob Kaufman's Beat poetry. Each work portrays two major conflicts that characterize black literature of the sixties. First, there is the overdetermined force of white patriarchy that places socioeconomic obstacles in the path of the black protagonist. Second, and as a direct reaction to white patriarchy, there is a struggle between adherence to and the rejection of black patriarchal and essentialist convictions that refuse a transracial, transgendered politics. I am interested in how black cosmopolitan characters and poetic voice deal with social and ethical issues that affect blacks as well as nonblacks.

JOHN A. WILLIAMS'S *THE MAN WHO CRIED I AM*: GENDER AND RACE

Williams's novel portrays an African American intellectual who tries to negotiate his professional career and his personal ethics. (A similar theme informs Armah's novel, although the setting in that case is postcolonial Ghana.) This dilemma creates psychological tensions and permits dialogism where dutiful commitment once reigned. Even though Armah's novel depicts a postcolonial Ghana and Williams's novel portrays an African American experience, both works dramatize a black intellectual who tries to negotiate his community's Negritude convictions with those of his personal desires. This dilemma creates a major psychological conflict within the character and affects a "motivated Signifyin(g)" between the forces of unyielding conformity and the liberating desire for openness and change. Similar to the film *Jungle Fever*, *The Man Who Cried I Am* has two major narrative levels that define the protagonist Max Reddick's unconscious and conscious voices. The two levels illustrate the tension between Max's Negritude and postNegritude beings.

The first level presents a college-educated, black novelist who gains his living by writing for a Harlem newspaper. Max falls in love with Lillian Patch, a black school teacher, but refuses to give up his literary ambitions in order to seek a better-paying job to support a middle-class life with Lillian Patch. Their lovemaking does not escape its biological consequences and Lillian becomes pregnant. Unable to persuade Max into a conventional marriage, or Lillian into a bohemian life with Max, the two try to find a qualified doctor to perform an abortion. Ironically, Max's white liberal friend recommends the doctor who performs abortions, but the doctor refuses to render this service to a black woman. Finally, Lillian gets her abortion and, quite tellingly, dies from internal bleeding as a consequence of the operation. The botched abortion and subsequent death of Lillian exemplify how patriarchy and racism affect the male protagonist Max. His inability to find better employment is yet another example of the overdetermined socioeconomic force of racist patriarchal conventions and norms which place obstacles in the path of both Max and Lillian.

Racist conventions denied Lillian a competent doctor to perform her abortion. Additionally, patriarchal conventions legally withhold the option of abortion from women like Lillian. The combined forces of racism and patriarchy force Lillian into accepting an incompetent abortion from which she dies.

After Lillian's death, Max acquires a job with a national magazine which sends him to report on the newly independent African nations. En route to Africa by way of Amsterdam, Max falls in love with Margrit, a white Dutch woman. In Europe, their love grows in a social environment free of covert racist reactions. Upon their arrival in New York City, they immediately marry. In the United States, the general racist climate of the sixties and the several racist actions they encounter impede the fruition of their marriage. Out of fear, Max begins to arm himself for a racial war. Margrit is incapable of understanding Max's self-defensive actions and the racism others direct at their romantic union. Reluctantly and dolefully, Margrit leaves Max and returns to Amsterdam.[9]

Max epitomizes the man who struggles against racism but is unable or unwilling to acknowledge his complicity in patriarchal forms of racism and/or bigotry. Max psychologically struggles between adherence to and the rejection of racial essentialism and patriarchal convictions. These convictions deny the possibility of a transracial womanist alternative that would provide Lillian, Margrit, and Max with a healthy social environment to express their humanity.

Lillian and Margrit symbolize the embodied and engendered discourse of the female Other to a Max who remains self-consumed with his unfulfilled manhood. His anger becomes a masculinist carnival that obscures any type of transracial, transgendered struggle against patriarchy and racism — the hegemonies that oppress, in different degrees, Max, Lillian, and Margrit.

In the Lillian and Max relationship, Max refuses to seek a full-time position and do his creative writing during the night. When Lillian becomes pregnant, she entreats Max with "Couldn't you write nights and work?" Max responds, "No. . . . I'm so damned full now. I'd hate to lose everything working. I feel free for the first time in my life. What would there be besides the *Democrat?* There aren't that many jobs downtown."[10] Max rejects a middle-class job at the *Democrat.* His rejection invariably forces Lillian to seek the abortion that results in her death. Ironically, Max's ideal reporting job is one that is with a white mainstream downtown firm; he rejects Lillian's proposal to continue his reporting job at the Harlem-based *Democrat.* Max honors a marriage union between the black writer and the white national press. Interestingly, Max's public desire to be wedded to the mainstream press is what prevents any successful wedding in his private life. Max correctly desires that America make use of his journalistic talents, but he is unable to consider the desires and needs of the two women he loves. Consequently, Lillian's death and Margrit's return to Holland move Max to a Negritude form of resistance that prevents gender equity and transracial intimacy. In this type of Negritude writing, womanism and transracial signifiers are of secondary importance to the black male protagonist, Max Reddick. Nonetheless, the passage of Lillian and Margrit produce psychological dissonance in Max and, thereby, cause additional Negritude subjective anguish.

Max's alter-ego is a signifying episodic voice that only Max hears. In the same way that society has questioned Max's manhood, the alter-ego refutes Max's professional success and reminds him of his private failures. Their debate reveals the limitations of Negritude subjectivity. Max's desire for professional success and public respect should elicit the cry of "I Am." But this cry excludes the equally important communal cry of "We Are." Max undergoes surgery and has been given sodium pentothal to anesthetize his senses. The drug also has the properties of a truth serum that permits Max's signifying alter-ego to begin a sermon on the blackness of Max's being.

> He was depressed. People whittling gleefully away at your flesh. . . . Just what did they do with the flesh: It was a little bit of dying, already, faster. Even with their clean sheets, drugs,

voluptuous nurses, flowers, diets, stainless steel tools, you were dying. But you knew that. . . . Why remember more than most the vast laboring distance so filled with internecine horror and commonplace death, the gift of that raving bitch, evolution, nature, now made gentle with the title, Mother, and keep crying I Am?[11]

Max's cry of "I Am" expresses utter disillusionment with those who determine the latitude and variance of his blackness. He has contempt for his medicinally clean and emotionally callous audience who pick away at his soul. But Max allows unbridled hatred and conceit to destroy two romantic unions. Max's sociopolitical awareness, like his morphine-ridden, cancerous body, remains a narcotized spectacle that resists a transgendered and womanist awakening.

PostNegritude angst also appears in certain postindependent black African novels. The Ghanaian novelist Ayi Kwei Armah is but one example of a West African writer who dramatizes a postNegritude disillusionment with postindependent Ghana. Similar in content to the postNegritude tensions in the life and nude photography of the Nigerian-born British photographer Rotimi Fani-Kayode who is discussed in "Renegotiating Black Masculinity," Armah's novel *Fragments*, which will be discussed later, explores the unfulfilled postindependent hopes of Baako Onipa, the protagonist.

According to my understanding of black intellectual and cultural history, which is not confined to canonical texts, a full-fledged assault on established black forms of subjectivity occurred when African nations and black diasporic communities gained a certain degree of independence from their former colonizers and slave masters. Henry Louis Gates describes the literary aspects of this independence.

The urge toward systematization of all of human knowledge, by which we characterize the Enlightenment, in other words led directly to the relegation of black people to a lower rung on the Great Chain of Being, an eighteenth century metaphor that arranged all of creation on the vertical scale from animals and plants and insects through man to angels and God himself. By 1750, the chain had become individualized; the human scale rose from "the lowliest Hottentot" (black South Africans) to the "glorious Milton and Newton." If blacks could write and publish imaginative literature, then they could, in effect, take a few giant steps up the Chain of Being, in a pernicious game of "Mother, May I?"[12]

With the rise of independent African nations, and the migration of black Caribbean communities to industrialized European metropolises, certain black writers and intellectuals realized that their work must portray the multiple experiences of black people. They equally recognized that their efforts should not present black humanity where it did not exist; to do otherwise would sanction further inhumane acts by black despots. Consequently, certain black artists and intellectuals, like Ralph Ellison, Ousmane Sembene, James Baldwin, and Ayi Kwei Armah, spoke about the hazards of racial essentialism. They were fully aware that socially constructed myths had been constructed as biological and religious facts and subsequently used to disenfranchise blacks of their civil rights.

The existence of African despots like Uganda dictator Idi Amin Dada (1971–1979) conflicts with the humanist hopes for postindependent Africa. Black African writers could no longer portray the leaders of independent African nations in a monolithic image as benevolent leaders. Africa was not the black person's idyllic refuge from European imperialism and the West's social inequities. This shift of consciousness in black writers and intellectuals indicates an instance of the postNegritude. Simon Mpondo explains this moment:

> A shift in consciousness, which was barely noticeable in colonial days, has become the trade mark of some of the best post-independence Negro-African writers. The contrary obsession has begun to assert itself and to prevail. The shift took the form of simple resistance to standardization, before turning into revulsion against it. . . . The new values are . . . mainly propounded in the works of the writers who came of age in the 1960's.
>
> The writers of the 1960's base their values on solid philosophical foundations. They believe that there are multiple and diverse merits in each and every parcel of human activity, and they trace the source of excellence back to that multiplicity and diversity.[13]

This type of black writing develops postNegritude. It portrays the desire for multiple and diverse forms of black subjectivity.

AYI KWEI ARMAH'S *FRAGMENTS*:
A STILL-DYING COLONIALISM

In *The Man Who Cried I Am*, the protagonist Max Reddick utters a singular cry of "I Am." Contrastingly, *Fragments* features a protagonist Baako Onipa who voices a collective cry that expresses the "I Am" awareness of self and the "We Are" awareness of his connecting to a multicultural community of marginal folk. The "We Are" is neither a spectacle between the alter-ego and a defeated Max, nor is it the result of a series of failed romantic unions. The "We Are" articulates a political criticism against a new black nation which has not implemented progressive social changes. It also speaks of the sociopsychical anguish of a community who refuses to give up their dreams for a better Ghanaian society.

In *Fragments*, Baako's mother Efua, his sister Araba, and his Uncle Foli champion the "I Am" values of Max Reddick in a materialistic sense. Because Baako has studied in the West, the community of "I Am"—his mother, sister, uncle, and neighbors—expect him to return and acquire western material objects. According to Efua, Araba, Uncle Foli, and the others, Baako's ability to acquire these objects signifies his financial wealth and wisdom. He has "been to" the West and has returned to provide a newly liberated African nation with the skills and riches to obtain western technology.

Baako's grandmother Naana, his expatriate, Puerto-Rican American girlfriend Juana, and his former art instructor Ocran comprise the community of "We Are." They oppose, in their respective way, the crass materialism of Efua, Araba, Uncle Foli, and the newly independent nation's race for western consumer goods. Naana preserves the ethical function of Akan tradition; Ocran articulates its philosophical opposition to self-aggrandizing "I Am" discourses; and Juana, a professional nurse and lover to Baako, assists Naana and Ocran as they attempt to heal a psychologically and spiritually fragmented Baako.

For example, Ocran attempts to persuade Baako to resist blind submission to an "I Am" norm that has made Ocran into a nonactional type of philosopher of the postmodern kind. Ocran says,

> Don't stop thinking, Onipa. You have a good mind; don't be afraid to use it. Stop thinking [and] you've done people wrong. . . . We all have relatives who want us to be like your Brempong—get them things that shout they're rich, they're

powerful. . . . The country's full of people dying to look down on everybody else.[14]

Ocran's speech articulates the voice of social humanism. Ocran's words direct Baako toward a social purpose which is at odds with the popular desire for objects of western modernity. In like manner, Juana nurses Baako's distraught will and warns him against trying to serve two masters—the urge for modern consumption and the vision of a postNegritude world order. This vision is expressed in the presence of Ocran and Baako and articulates their philosophical connection to the other.

> Ocran looked from Baako to Juana, [with] incomprehension in his face. She did not want the thread to be broken, so she said, "It can be a terrifying conflict, if you see the need to help relatives, though, and also do something useful in the larger sense. There are two communities, really, and they don't coincide. It's not an emptiness you need to cover up with things. You are not a businessman."[15]

Juana describes the communities of the "I Am" and "We Are."

The "I Am" discourse of worldly success destroyed Max's romance with Lillian and later caused the rupture of his marriage with Margrit. Max consistently refused to acknowledge his failed romances, and he fended off his alter-ego's criticisms of his self-pity in a post-Civil Rights America. Similar discourses of desire for worldly success confront Baako. These desires, however, are articulated by other individuals whose needs momentarily destroy Baako's psychological well-being.

In counterpoint to Max's terminal cancerous body, Baako psyche cannot survive the seemingly endless "I Am" cries by the postcolonial Ghanaians who surround him. Fortunately, he later recognized that their misguided expectations and personal greed produce governmental corruption. Unfortunately, Max never fully recognizes that his desire for mainstream recognition is self-destructive, even though this is personified by his rotting, cancerous body. Baako, on the other hand, meets with the "been to" discourses of "I Am" of the West and veers towards the possible "We Are" of the world.

In Baako's move towards the possible, he becomes caught between the teeth of two constructions of black middle class heroics. Here lies the postNegritude landscape of possibilities. PostNegritude positions itself at the juncture where Negritude struggles with racist paradigms.

Baako's grandmother reassures the reader that he will not remain in his present psychologically distraught state—a type of fragmented hero of the postmodern. Naana states,

> When I go I will protect him if I can, and if my strength is not enough, I will seek out stronger spirits and speak to their souls of his need for them.[16]

Naana's farewell describes how a multitude of other spirits will protect Baako's travel between misguided Negritude desires and postmodern fragmentation.

There exists a major difference between the blackness of a post-Negritude and a raceless postmodernity. PostNegritude rejects the inevitable fragmentation of black identity to produce multiplicity. PostNegritude advances the existence of blackness as an always constant mix of the African with the European experience. Neither experience should be seen as totalizing and, therein, erasing or silencing the other. Homi Bhabha explains,

> The fragmentation of identity is often celebrated as a kind of pure anarchic liberalism or voluntarism, but I prefer to see it as a recognition of the importance of the alienation of the self in the construction of forms of solidarity.
>
> It is only by losing the sovereignty of the self that you can gain the freedom of a politics that is open to the nonassimilationist claims of cultural difference. The crucial feature of the new awareness is that it doesn't need to totalise in order to legitimate political action or cultural practice. That is the real issue.[17]

Thus, in comparing the black protagonists Max Reddick in *The Man Who Cried I Am* and Baako Onipa in *Fragments*, one finds the former is blinded by patriarchal Negritude which prevents Max from loving (as opposed to having sex with) any woman regardless of her race. In the latter case, Ghana's postcolonial reality bewilders Baako who, like Ghana, is unable to escape a colonial past and the neocolonial system that prevents societal progress. The psychological fragmentation of each protagonist does not predict the dissolution of all progressive forms of black subjectivity; it merely infers that multiple subject positions must be realized. This is evident in the multiple-voiced Baako and the self-destruction of cancerous Max. Likewise, in Adrienne Kennedy's *The Funnyhouse of a Negro* there is a polyphony of voices emitted from the fragmented mind of a black woman whose Negritude and postNegritude selves are in battle.

ADRIENNE KENNEDY'S
THE FUNNYHOUSE OF A NEGRO

The Funnyhouse of a Negro opened in Greenwich Village at the East End Theater on January 14, 1964. "Sarah the Negro" is the name of the black female protagonist in this play. Sarah suffers an emotional breakdown from internalizing society's racial norms that demand that the individual be of one nation, one race, and one sex. Like Baako Onipa in *Fragments*, the female protagonist is emotionally distressed because societal conventions refuse to acknowledge her important self-discovery.

Sarah is the daughter of a dark-complexioned father and an "almost" white mother. She despises her father because he is the source of her pale-yellow skin and frizzy hair. Ironically, she loses her hair as the play progresses; thus, one defect is lost and another is gained.

Sarah has two imaginary white identities who express her racial and class desires. She is intermittently the Duchess of Hapsburg and the Queen of England. Both personalities represent Sarah's assimilation of European culture and her wish to escape middle-class mediocrity. Unfortunately, other personalities assert themselves within Sarah. She changes into two sociopolitical martyrs—Jesus Christ and Patrice Lumumba, the first prime minister of Zaire. Both men threatened the political status quo and were subsequently murdered by its policing agents.

The play also features her "Mother" who represents the universal "almost white" woman who is also the mother of the Duchess and Queen Victoria. Ironically, the father of these two European aristocrats is Patrice Lumumba whom the "Mother" regrets having married because he is a black man:

> Black man, black man, I never should have let a black man put his hands on me. The wild black beast raped me and now my skull is shining.[18]

Before the Mother has expressed her regrets, the Duchess and the Queen reveal that their father was a black man. Because Sarah imagines herself as the white aristocratic Duchess and Queen, their revelation of black ancestry problematizes Sarah's rejection of her dark-complexioned father. The tension between the Duchess and Queen's celebration of blackness and Sarah's denial expresses the psychological importance in recognizing one's multiracial identity. Thus, a postNegritude reading of Sarah's mental instability views her psychological dilemma as an indication of the complex nature of black diasporic racial identity. The Negritude cultural politics of the sixties demand that Sarah deny her multiracial heritage. Thus, if she is mentally well she is African, and if she is psychologically unstable, she is European. Neither paradigm admits that she can be multicultural and, perhaps, multiracial as well.

The other characters include Raymond, Sarah's Jewish lover and the Funnyhouse Man, and Landlady, who is intermittently Mrs. Conrad and the Funnyhouse Lady. These two characters, Raymond and the Landlady, end the play with different tales about Sarah's biological father. The Landlady says, "Her father hung himself in a Harlem hotel when Patrice Lumumba died." Raymond offers a negative picture of her father:

> Her father never hung himself in a Harlem hotel when Patrice Lumumba was murdered. I know the man. He is a doctor, married to a white whore. He lives in the city in a room with European antiques, photographs of Roman ruins, walls of books and oriental carpets. Her father is a nigger who eats his meals on a white glass table. [19]

This contradictory nature reflects the nature of the play and the statements made by its characters. As I have mentioned earlier, Sarah's dislike for her black father and her wish to be accepted by the symbols of European aristocracy refer to the integration movement of the late fifties and early sixties. Sarah's fragmented identities result from her interracial college education which is metaphorically described as a spatial-temporal relationship with Queen Victoria:

> I am an English major, as my mother was when she went to school in Atlanta. My father majored in social work. I am graduated from a city college and have occasional work in libraries. . . . I write poetry, filling white page after white page with imitations of Edith Sitwell. It is my dream to live in

rooms with European antiques and my Queen Victoria, photographs of Roman ruins, walls of books, a piano, oriental car-
pets, and to eat my meals on a white glass table.[20]

Sarah is a product of her parents and the results of aspiring to images of the dominant culture which consumes Sarah and spits her out
in fragmented spittle. This spittle taints Patrice Lumumba because he is
also one of Sarah's selves. Lumumba states that he is "a nigger of two
generations" and later, he will connect Sarah to "the generation born at
the turn of the century and the generation born before the depression."
Sarah speaks to the audience behind the mask of Lumumba. We learn
that she lives in New York City in a brownstone in the West Nineties.
Through Lumumba she attacks the black middle class who aspires to
material luxuries and consumption for the sake of it:

> It is also my nigger dreams for my friends to eat their meals on
> white glass tables. . . . My friends will be white. I need them as
> an embankment to keep me from reflecting too much upon
> the fact that I am Patrice Lumumba. . . . My white friends,
> like myself, will be shrewd intellectuals and anxious for death.
> . . . For if I did not despise myself then my hair would not
> have fallen and if my hair had not fallen then I would not
> have bludgeoned my father's face with the ebony mask.[21]

"Nigger dreams" and the American Dream are synonymous because
both lead to what every middle-class family should "eat on" if they want
to enjoy membership among "friends." Lumumba uses "white" as a
marker that signifies membership in a group anxious for death. This
group is not a racially white group, but they share white values. The
group is black like the ebony mask of the bearer of this warning to the
educated black middle class. Sarah, in the mask of Patrice Lumumba,
articulates her self-hatred. The "frizzy" hair which she began to lose
when she entered the play is now lost. Like her mother, Sarah has a
bald skull.[22] Yet, her mother did not enter the asylum until all her hair
had fallen; Sarah has lost hair on her crown and temples. With hair
remaining on both sides of her head, she resembles a clown. If we are to
understand Sarah's hair loss as a mark of her growing insanity, then we
should recognize that the mental selves function as clues to Sarah's
schizoid world and its meaning. In the mask of Jesus, Sarah describes
how her Jesus-self tries to escape being black. Disguised, he will go to

Africa using the name Albert Saxe Coburg and Queen Victoria. He intends to kill his black father, Patrice Lumumba:

> Jesus: Through my apocalypses and my raging sermons I have tried so to escape him, through God Almighty I have tried to escape being black. . . . I am going to Africa and kill this black man named Patrice Lumumba. Why? Because all my life I believed my Holy Father to be God, but now I know that my father is a black man. I have no fear for whatever I do, I will do it in the name of God, I will do it in the name of Albert Saxe Coburg, in the name of Victoria, Queen Victoria.[23]

Sarah's schizoid world reflects the international experience of people of African ancestry. Sarah's mental condition is an allegorical representation of the psychological experience of westernized black folk. Sarah's world is marked by racism, self-hatred and moral disillusion. Still, she retains an element of the heroic because Sarah's Patrice Lumumba self continues to resist. None of Sarah's other "selves" are allowed to escape Lumumba; even though he has been murdered, the other "selves" cannot escape Lumumba's spirit.

> Duchess and Jesus: My father isn't going to let us alone. Our father isn't going to let us alone, our father is the darkest of us all, my mother was the fairest, I am in between, but my father is the darkest of them all. He is a black man. Our father is the darkest of them all. He is a black man. My father is a dead man.[24]

Sarah's various "selves" conclude in an affirming chorus that connects Jesus, Lumumba, the Duchess, and Queen Victoria to a black Negro. Their only escape from this consciousness would be his death. His physical death has not dulled his spiritual presence and the other selves are quick to admit this: "But he is dead. And he keeps returning. Then he is not dead, Yes, he is dead, but dead he comes knocking at my door."[25]

As mentioned earlier, the Landlady and Raymond conclude the play with different statements about Sarah's father. The Landlady and Raymond offer the audience two contradictory images of Sarah's black father. The Landlady says "Her father hung himself in a Harlem hotel when Patrice Lumumba died."[26] Raymond's version paints the father in a more negative light.[27] According to Raymond, her father is an enemy of Negritude solidarity because his qualities are individualistic and apolitical. Sarah must battle with both patriarchal suicidal images and, ultimately, both patriarchs will strangle Sarah's spiritual and physical selves.

Throughout the play, Sarah has denied her Patrice Lumumba self because his black presence forces her to recognize a black heredity and, therein, a Patrice Lumumba-like social responsibility to uplift the black race. Consistent with Sarah's displeasure with her black kinky hair which she loses to baldness, and consistent with Sarah's rejection of her dark-complexioned father, she rejects social responsibility and, therein, incurs a more fatal loss—her suicide by self-hanging. The suicide acts as closure to the play and points to Sarah's twisted complicity in the death of Negritude impositions on her multiracial and multicultural transgendered selves.

Critic Marc Robinson describes Funnyhouse as resulting from Kennedy's visit to Africa. He writes,

> Naturally the African sojourn strengthened Kennedy's consciousness of her race—instilling pride in a history that she had barely known before her trip, offering an alternative to the self-hatred she developed at Ohio State.[28]

The alternative that is offered provides Kennedy with a postNegritude tension that recognizes African history and pride in two of its new political leaders—Kwame Nkrumah and Patrice Lumumba. This recognition, however, does not totally erase her racist American experience nor does it make her adopt the prevaling Negritude ideals that many of her contemporaries held. Robinson explains,

> But she never thought in purely racial terms. Blackness and Africanness were abstractions to her. . . . her characters struggle with the meaning of blackness, but Kennedy should never be thought of as a "black playwright" or a writer speaking for [only] her race or somehow putting a generalized black heritage on stage. Perhaps this refusal to speak impersonally about black history explains Kennedy's isolation from other black writers; politics in her work, and in her life, has been simply one force among many affecting the consciousness of a character also assailed by the implications of a place,

upbringing, a family, and a lifetime of mundane, quotidian obligations.[29]

Bob Kaufman's surrealist poems express similar disenchantment with monopoles of blackness which place obstacles in the path of a postNegritude blackness. While Adrienne Kennedy voices her opinions through the image of mixed-race Sarah, Kaufman occasionally uses his African-Jewish American self as the subject in his poems.

BOB KAUFMAN: SELECTED POETIC BROODINGS ON THE POSTNEGRITUDE

Bob Garnell Kaufman was born on April 18, 1925 in New Orleans, Louisiana. It is widely believed that he was one of fourteen children from a marriage between a German-Jewish poolroom owner and a Black Martinican woman. His father died when Kaufman was still in his youth. "At 13 he left home to go to sea and sailed for 20 years with the merchant marine. During those years, the older crewmen imparted to him a taste for literature."[30] Kaufman's taste for literature grew into an interest in writing prose poetry. He left the merchant marine and married Eileen.

Kaufman's German-Jewish father and his entrance into the merchant marine at the young age of thirteen are more legend than truth. Maria Damon's research refutes many of the claims about Bob Kaufman's early life. Damon interviewed Bob's brother George who stated that their paternal grandfather was half-Jewish and that their father was a Pullman porter and "mother came from an old, well-known Black New Orleans family, the Vignes."[31] This news might shatter certain bloodline, biracial claims about Kaufman's genealogy. It, however, does little to dampen the poetic imagination of a biracial Jewish-African American heritage that Kaufman incorporates in his poetry.

At the close of the fifties, Bob Kaufman had attracted notoriety as a gifted but mentally imbalanced poet. Jazz musicians and Beat writers respected Kaufman as a poet, even though he was difficult to get along with. This group of Beat artists frequented cafes in San Francisco and Manhattan's East Village, and jazz clubs on the West and East coasts. During this cultural period, Bob Kaufman and LeRoi Jones were some of the most influential African American Beat writers in a group of predominantly white men. Both Kaufman and Jones wrote jazz-influenced poetry and helped publish many of the world-renowned Beat poets of this period. In Arnold Adoff's *Poetry of Black America*, Adoff writes that Bob Kaufman

> was a leading poet during the 1950s . . . "renaissance." He was influential in the development of white "beat" poets such as Allen Ginsberg, Gregory Corso, and Lawrence Ferlinghetti. Bob Kaufman had earned great respect for his work in England and France before it became well known in this country.[32]

In an article appearing in the *San Francisco Examiner*, Tony Seymour writes that

> The original Be-Bop Man, Bob Kaufman was an unpublicized driving force among a group of internationally known writers including Allen Ginsberg, Jack Kerouac, Lawrence Ferlinghetti, William Burroughs, and Gregory Corso.[33]

Even though the fifties witnessed the first wave of jazz-poetry performances, Langston Hughes and Vachel Lindsay had written poetry influenced by the popular music of the 1920s. When literary critics discuss jazz-poetry and proclaim, in high notes, that Kenneth Patchen was the first to attempt jazz-poetry integration, they overlook the earlier experiments that were first attempted by Vachel Lindsay and then Langston Hughes, and brought to fruition by poets such as Bob Kaufman.[34] In the late fifties, Kaufman began writing his poems on discarded pieces of paper. His published poetry first appeared in *Beatitude*, a San Francisco poetry magazine that he cofounded with Allen Ginsberg, Bill Margolis, and John Kelley in 1959.[35] Later, Lawrence Ferlinghetti's City Lights Press published three of Kaufman's poems as broadsides. Several years later, Kaufman's poems were published in his three books of collected poems titled, respectively, *Solitudes Crowded With Loneliness* (New Directions, 1965), *The Golden Sardine* (City Lights, 1967), and *The Ancient Rain* (New Directions, 1981).

Kaufman's jazz-poetry performance resembled that of a mad African griot the purpose of whose memory and oral delivery was to entertain and educate his tribal community. In griot-like fashion, Kaufman's performance related contemporary social history to his tribe of Beats. His prose style and invective tone lash out at America's inhumanity. His poem "San Francisco Beat" is one illustration of his urban griot style.

Jazz cops with ivory nightsticks,
Leaning on the heads of imitation Negroes,
Selling ice cubes to returned virgins,
Wrapping velvet Band-Aids, over holes
In the arms of heaven-headed junkies.[36]

In this particular poem, Kaufman describes his everyday confrontations with the local police and his ritual use of intravenous drugs. His performance amused a community of drug users who, like Bob, sought narcotic heavens. Kaufman is the jazz-poet *cum* griot of the Beat community's drug culture.

Unfortunately, this Black urban griot and Jewish jazzy cantor had to endure such dehumanizing racist rituals as police brutality, imprisonment, and forced electroshock therapy.[37] These rituals were all too familiar to black men like Kaufman. In a 1976 interview with Tony Seymour of the *San Francisco Examiner*, Bob's wife, Eileen Kaufman, described Bob as the *bête noire* of the San Francisco police. She recalled that

The police tried to keep Bob down a lot. He baited them a lot. Since he was so vivacious [and black] and dominated the whole scene, he appeared as the leader. They arrested him. He was more frank than a lot of people about the police and he'd say anything.[38]

In 1960, the Kaufmans moved to New York City where Bob, Eileen, and their infant son, Parker, took up residence in the East Village. They added to an already large, multiracial group of bohemians who rubbed shoulders with first generation Eastern European immigrants. LeRoi Jones and his wife Hettie Coleman also took up residence in the East Village. The Kaufman family, like the Jones-Coleman family, suffered racial insults from the East Village old-timers. Parker was attacked and spat upon by some of the newly arrived wannabe Americans.[39] These racist aggressions surely soured Kaufman's heart but could not silence his pen. He continued writing poetry and within a year his poems were published in a 1961 New Directions poetry anthology. In England, he was nominated for the 1961 Guinness Poetry Award. The same year, Fawcett published his coauthored novel (with Lou Morheim) *Isolation Booth* and, the following year, Muller Press published it for the British market.

In 1963, Kaufman served time on Riker's Island for drug posses-
sion, and on his release, he returned to his original North Beach stomp-
ing grounds. Arriving in San Francisco, Kaufman found that the North
Beach had drastically changed its attitude toward him. In addition to
the eviction notice that welcomed him on his return, he was *persona
non grata* in many of the coffeehouses where he had read poetry. According to many of the North Beach merchants, Kaufman was a Black
troublemaker. His literary success in Europe and on the East Coast had
not changed their opinion of him. In response to their callous treatment, Kaufman composed "Oct. 5th, 1963" as a letter to the editor of
the *San Francisco Chronicle.* "I am writing these lines to the non-
people. One thing is certain I am not white. Thank God for that. It
makes everything else bearable."[40]

Kaufman's 1963 return marked the beginning of a tragic decade
that witnessed political assassinations[41] and the fire-bombing of the Six-
teenth Street Baptist Church in Birmingham, Alabama.[42] Ironically,
1963 marked one hundred years since Lincoln signed the Emancipa-
tion Proclamation. As cited in the above quotation, Kaufman was con-
tented with one fact, that he could tell the *Examiner's* readership "one
thing is certain I am not white. Thank God for that. It makes everything
else bearable."

KAUFMAN'S POSTNEGRITUDE POETICS

Many of Kaufman's poems center on three basic issues: racism, imperialism, and the spiritual force of jazz. He often uses a biblical prose
structure to explore these issues. In these particular poems, he criticizes
America's mistreatment of African Americans and, by extension, its racist practices abroad. Additionally, his political poems criticize atomic
warfare and Nazi death camps. This specific group of poems calls for an
apocalypse which, Kaufman believes, will liberate blacks and other oppressed people. Kaufman's poem "Benediction" exemplifies his inter-
nationalist interests, his robust anger at America's inhumanity to people
of color, and his hope for an apocalyptic end.

"Benediction," a poem written in the early sixties, borrows the structure of a religious rite in which good deeds are dedicated to God.
Kaufman perverts this ritual by listing racial and social injustices, which
he offers to America. Consequently, Kaufman's Americanized "Benedic-

tion" tells about the ritualistic offering of Black children and burning Japanese babies to a hungry America. The first stanza of the poem reads:

Pale brown Moses went down to Egypt land
To let somebody's people go.
Keep him out of Florida, no UN there:
The poor governor is all alone,
With six hundred thousand illiterates.[43]

Kaufman refers to "Florida" as a land of *un-united* people. The "Pale brown Moses" refers to the northern Black civil-rights workers. These northern Blacks, according to Kaufman, will travel to the South to help liberate southern Blacks.

The second stanza enumerates the Ku Klux Klan's racial lynchings and cross burnings. In a satiric mode, Kaufman forgives America for its racist actions, because such crude acts express America's impulsive hunger for tender, young, black bodies. Kaufman writes,

America, I forgive you. . . I forgive you
Nailing black Jesus to an imported cross
Every six weeks in Dawson, Georgia,
America, I forgive you . . . I forgive you
Eating black children, I know your hunger.[44]

Kaufman thus describes America's Jeffrey Dahmer-like hunger.[45]

As mentioned earlier, Kaufman links America's history of domestic racism to similar histories of racial oppression. Consequently, his poem "Benediction" makes reference to the use of atomic warfare against Japanese people. In "Benediction" the stanzas associate America's racism toward Blacks with its World War II use of the atomic bomb against Japanese civilians. Again Kaufman ironically defends this racial hunger, but never allows his audience to forget America's histories of unrestrained inhumanity to people of color. He writes,

America, I forgive you . . . I forgive you
Burning Japanese babies defensively—
I realize how necessary it was.[46]

Kaufman's invective prose presents a "greedy-as-they-want-to-be" America. He explains that the nation's health depends on these racial sacrifices. Then he excuses this racist hunger that demands the eating

of Black children and the burning of Japanese babies. Kaufman acquits
America and informs America that,

> Your ancestor had beautiful thoughts in his brain.
> His descendants are experts in real estate.
> Your generals have mushrooming visions.
> Every day your people get more and more
> Cars, televisions, sickness, death dreams.
> You must have been great
> Alive.[47]

Kaufman's "Benediction" shares a close resemblance to Jean
Toomer's "Brown River, Smile." Both poems seek a spiritual alternative
to America's racist and combative nature. In the poem "Brown River,
Smile," Toomer tells us that

> The old gods, led by an inverted Christ,
> A shaved Moses, a blanched Lemur,
> And a moulting thunderbird,
> Withdrew into the distance and soon died,
> Their dust and seed falling down
> To fertilize the five regions of America.
> We are waiting for a new God.[48]

Toomer acknowledges western technological advances but is quick to
add that such advances "died congested in machinery." Kaufman's
"Benediction" continues Toomer's call for America's spiritual renewal.
When Toomer envisioned an apocalypse that would bring forth a new
America, Kaufman predicted America's racist hunger would bring
about such a rebirth through an apocalypse. When Toomer spoke to a
nation after the First World War, Kaufman spoke to a nation still hun-
gering after having witnessed the Nazi death camps and the human
carnage that followed atomic warfare.

Kaufman wished for the destruction of the materialist world, but
he did not seek a state-controlled government. Kaufman envisioned a
utopian state in which art, poetry, and music, preferably jazz, would
surface like a phoenix out of the ashes of burning crosses and atomic
bombs. In his poem "Believe, Believe," he paints this new world order:

> Believe in this. Young apple seeds,
> In blue skies, radiating young breast,

> Not in blue-suited insects,
> Infesting society's garments.[49]

Kaufman saw change through belief in the metaphysical. He condemned the technocrats and scientists for having brought the world into the atomic age. Kaufman, Toomer, and the American Transcendentalists viewed men of science, industry, and commerce as the scoundrels of modern times. Kaufman had no place for these types in his garden of jazzy delights. Unlike the early Transcendentalists, however, Kaufman envisioned an urban heaven where multiracial hipsters read jazz-poetry on the sidewalks, in cafes, and in police stations. Kaufman wanted us to believe in his drug-induced dreams.

> Believe in the swinging sounds of jazz,
> Tearing the night into intricate shreds,
> Putting it back together again,
> In cool logical patterns,
> Not in the sick controllers,
> Who created only the Bomb.[50]

Where Toomer attacked industry, Kaufman attacked nuclear technology. Kaufman warned us not to heed the gods of the material world, because they would lead to destruction.

> Let the voices of dead poets
> Ring louder in your ears
> Than the screechings mouthed
> In mildewed editorials.
> Listen to the music of centuries,
> Rising above the mushroom time.[51]

In like manner, Toomer's "Brown River, Smile" ends with an encouraging announcement:

> It is a new America,
> To be spiritualized by each new American.[52]

Kaufman and Toomer called on a new group—the new American and the young apple seeds. Both poets saw a phoenix rising above "the inverted Christ" of Toomer, and "the mushroom time" of Kaufman. Their poetic use of black music and religious imagery counterbalance America's postwar fixation with technology and international commerce. Kaufman and Toomer are each the pale-brown Moses who observe a world that consumes golden calves but remains hungry for more Black children and burnt Japanese babies.

In the late 1960s, the Black Arts movement rejected the same bourgeois American values that Kaufman rejected almost ten years earlier. Nonetheless, the Black Arts movement did not embrace Kaufman, because his work did not immediately reflect the singular racial concerns of the Black Art Movement. In Kaufman's prose poem "Second April," he expresses his inability to reconcile this black and white binarism—a racial dilemma that registers people and their ethics as either black or white things. He informs us that

> they watch,
> we hide, sneak, make mad in corners,
> that's the thing,
> a thing world watches things,
> world, that's a thing,
> my negro suit has jew stripes,
> my yarmaka [sic] was lost in a flash flood
> while i mattered with navajos about peyote.[53]

Similar to the mixed-race character Sarah in Adrienne Kennedy's *Funnyhouse of a Negro*, Kaufman rejected racial dualism because he knew that his "negro suit has jew stripes." He still was able to write poems that spoke about America's race-warped hunger.

Unfortunately, there has been little interest in Kaufman's postNegritude work. This is especially unfortunate since his poetry, like Malcolm X's late political agenda, links black consciousness to an international awareness. If one traced the careers of Jean Toomer, Langston Hughes, and many of the best Black Art poets, we discover that their creative work ends where Bob Kaufman's vision began. Similar to Max Reddick in *The Man Who Cried I Am*, Baako Onipa in *Fragments*, and Sarah in *Funnyhouse of A Negro*, the voice in Bob Kaufman's poetry describes a postNegritude poetics of transracial, transnational awareness of the world community.

AFTER SOWING POSTNEGRITUDE LITERARY SEEDS

In concluding this backward look at Negritude literature on the edge, the two novels, one play, and poems portray the tragic limits of Negritude in post-1950s Black America and post-Independent Ghana (Africa). The first three works have major protagonists who commit social transgressions such as in Max's interracial marriage, Baako's denouncing government corruption and personal greed, and Sarah's racial self-hatred and suicide. Bob Kaufman's poetry echoes Sarah's biracial angst, Baako's disgust with governmental corruption, and Max's fear of an impending international racial war. The protagonists in the two novels and play, and Kaufman's poetic voice, reject racial and governmental conventions which have psychologically dehumanized the protagonists and the poet. Their writing serves a disruptive, liberating political role as well as an affirmative personal one.

The four writers construct despairing images of their black protagonists who attempt to trangress Negritude and other dominant social conventions which limit their desires. The writers use literature to covertly criticize the hegemony of white patriarchal institutions which deny certain black experiences. The authors negotiate an uncomfortable space between racial essentialism and patriarchy. Their works forecast the future postNegritudinal transgressions that certain cultural workers will employ against patriarchal and monolithic subject positions.

For instance, the 1969 and 1978 reprints of Zora Neale Hurston's 1937 novel *Their Eyes Were Watching God* point to the growing importance of black womanist fiction. In 1969, the Negro Universities Press reissued the novel for, perhaps, a black academic market created by recently established Black Studies programs. In 1978, almost a decade later, the predominantly white University of Illinois Press reprinted Hurston's debut novel for consumption by a crossover market composed of black literature and Women's Studies courses. The two reprints indicate the marketability of this type of black literature even though the novel was initially published in 1937. An inclusive black feminism (which I also refer to as womanism) is an essential part of the postNegritude. The social experiences and creativity of black women has been in the vanguard of pioneering progressive forms of blackness. The empowerment of black females like Anita Hill provides black life with a polyphonic chorus composed of multifaceted faces.

On a cautionary note, one should keep in mind that tracing a singular trajectory of award-winning African American literature obscures how book publishing participates in capital-intensive, interconnected processes that rely heavily on marketing, advertising, editing, and the good will of the literary critics and teachers. The publications of black womanists and postNegritude theorists do not escape these requirements, but they can avoid being determined by the destructive processes that could create a unique type of black feminism and postNegritude creativity. Production, distribution, and consumption should never be a unilateral proposition between a black critical center and its many peripheries.

Recently, international black artists such as the African American Marlon Riggs and the African British photographer Rotimi Fani-Kayode, have resisted heterosexist hegemony and broadened the definition of black masculinity to encompass their respective gay masculine visions. "Renegotiating Black Masculinity," the next chapter, discusses how their work negotiates the inclusion of a gay black masculine subjectivity that resists the determinism of white patriarchy and rigid forms of black nationalism. In this type of black art, a postNegritude consciousness negotiates a place for a transnational and transexual understanding of black cultural identity. This revised mode of black creative production relies on womanist modes of production and reception.

4

RENEGOTIATING
BLACK MASCULINITY

I n recent years, African American creative artists have reworked the visual and literary construction of black sexuality. These revised configurations are present in black-oriented films, videos, photographs, mixed media, and literature produced in the United States and Great Britain. One needs only to view some of the works by the African American filmmakers Michelle Parkerson and Marlon Riggs, the London-based Afro-British filmmaker Isaac Julien, and the deceased Nigerian expatriate London photographer Rotimi Fani-Kayode.

Among the many gay and lesbian African American writers the names of James Baldwin, Samuel R. Delany, and Audre Lorde are now established in the African-American literary canon. These artists have produced black art that disrupts the hegemony of an erotic colonialist and heterosexist gaze upon the black body. Such a colonialist gaze frames Leni Riefenstahl's pseudoethnographic photographs in *The Last of the Nuba* (1973) and Robert Mapplethorpe's homoerotic portraits of black men in his *Black Book* (1986). Besides these more obvious examples of the colonizing gaze, there exist the more complex and slippery examples that receive a more mixed reception. The controversial reception of Trinh T. Minh-Ha's abstract film *Reassemblage* (1982) illustrates how a critique of the colonialist gaze might be perceived as a celebration. Consequently, the manner in which black bodies have been visually constructed and exchanged for erotic and political consumption is of theoretical importance. Additionally, one must recognize that certain

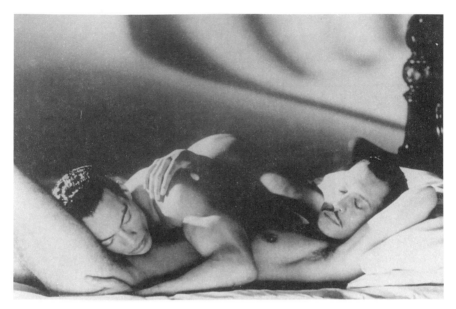

Figure 15. Isaac Julien's *Looking For Langston*: Two nude black men embrace in a reclining position. Photo courtesy BFI Stills, Posters and Designs.

works, like *Reassemblage*, require that the critic pose different questions when assessing the artistic and political merits of any work.

The documentary framing of black sexuality calls forth a variety of modes of reception whose selection depends on how negotiations are exchanged. An onlooker can resist, assimilate, or perform a combination of the two when interpreting a work's meaning and worth. The recent controversy over Robert Mapplethorpe's photographs and the rap group 2 Live Crew's lyrics shows that visual and auditory reception is neither a fixed entity nor a simple interpretive process of encoding and decoding. Sociopsychological factors and one's individual perception determine what constitutes the erotic, the political, and the pornographic. Thus, the interpretation of the sexualized or nonsexualized black subject requires an interdisciplinary mode of cultural inquiry. I suggest a comparative approach in which interpretation discerns the text, its production, and its reception of sexualized or nonsexualized black subjects. It is also important to determine how artists, multinational corporations, and consumers psychically and socially resist, appropriate, and assimilate certain types of sexual narratives. We must employ, as Miriam Hansen argues,

A concept of *experience* which not only is the opposite of so-cially constructed signs and systems of representation but, rather, mediates between individual perception and social determinations, and emphatically entails memory and an awareness of its historical diminishment.[1]

Thus, any womanist alternative tradition must not hesitate to critically assess how black artists negotiate between racist and sexist individual perception and its socially determined correlation. The tradition must equally assess the processes of resistance that construct an emphatic womanism. Both moves entail memory and an awareness of its histori-cal diminishment. As stated in my earlier writings on postNegritude and womanism, I borrow the term "womanism" from Alice Walker who describes it as a female-centered activity. She writes,

A woman who loves other women, sexually and/or non-sexually. Appreciates and prefers women's culture, women's emotional flexibility . . . and women's strength. Sometimes loves individual men, sexually and/or nonsexually. Commit-ted to survival and wholeness of entire people, male *and* female. Not a separatist, except periodically, for health. Tradi-tionally universalist, as in: "Mama, why are we brown, pink, and yellow, and our cousins are white, beige, and black?" . . . Loves struggle. Loves the Folk. Loves herself. Regardless. Womanist is to feminist as purple is to lavender.[2]

Womanism espouses a feminism that equally considers issues of gender, race, class, ethnicity, and sexual orientation. In essence, womanism is a *profane mode of feminism*. The term "profane" expresses that the subject is "Nonreligious in subject matter, form, or use; secu-lar."[3] Profane is to respectable, as womanist is to feminist, as feminist is to masculinist, as movement is to reflection, as stagnation is to the fluid, as an ever-changing movement demands a form of resistance that per-mits negotiation.

In the early seventies, black women and men started to criticize patriarchal practices in and outside the black community. Black gay activists took to the streets and registered their pride in annual marches throughout the United States. Black participation in the Gay and Les-bian Pride marches increased the African American community's awareness of the existence of sexual diversity within the black commu-nity. The growing presence of proud black gays and lesbians not only

demystified the dominant image of black America as a strictly heterosexual entity, but provided visual proof that the black homosexual community was equally proud of its racial heritage.

By the 1980s, African Americans came to realize, though there
are many who will never accept, that there are prominent African
American leaders and artists who would no longer be silenced by the
hegemony of a heterosexual blackness. Many perceived that black gay
and lesbian activism would be detrimental to the black community.
This anxiety exacerbated the past fears that racists would use the
newly emergent black gay, lesbian, and feminist voices to further dehumanize black people. Reactionary forces within the black community increasingly appropriated the master narratives of homophobia
and misogyny in their nationalist calls for racial solidarity. The black
gay and lesbian communities criticized the backwardness of certain
black leaders and artists. They called for a true black solidarity and
looked for the community to support their celebration of blackness.
Consequently, a few progressive black artists like James Baldwin,
Audre Lorde, and Samuel R. Delany seized upon this dilemma and
expressed it in their literary works. A multilayered black creative paradigm unfolded and expressed the internal and external forms of sexual
oppression. This reworked paradigm creates spaces and free zones of
discourse for the formerly profane black subjects who are now empowered with voice and presence.

Following the move to de-center the sexual construction of the
black subject, black cultural criticism must interpret the sociological
and psychical forces that determine this sexualized reassemblage of
what was once invisible and unvoiced. Such forces include but are
not limited to the artist-producer, the apparatuses of production and
consumption, and the audience's *imagined* and *experienced* identification with the *black* sexualized subject of creation at any socio-
historical moment.

BLACK MASCULINITY AND POSTNEGRITUDE
GAY INTERVENTIONS

Marlon Riggs' *Tongues Untied* (1989) articulates two identification
modes that intersect and result in the production of "differing forms of
reception." One might view the film as a celebration of blackness, or a
celebration of homosexuality. A womanist reading would permit the
film to celebrate its intended message—affirming the black-gay experi-

ence. As stated earlier, I intend to discuss a profane mode of imagining black sexuality by focusing on the filmic and extrafilmic construction of African American gay men in *Tongues Untied.*

I am not arguing for a singular notion of realism. However, I would like to suggest that social and psychical experiences can constitute several formations of the "real." Each form meets at different historical moments and contests hegemony, or aligns with a hegemonic form and thereby creates a hybridized, hegemonic order of the "real." Therefore "womanism" should not be viewed as ignoring the importance of other *lived* experiences such as class. Womanism, however, contests the destructive elements in certain masculinist and nationalist forms of subjectivity. A few illustrations of these destructive forms are present in the standup humor of Eddie Murphy and Andrew Dice Clay, and in the lyrics of the groups "2 Live Crew" and "Guns and Roses."

Tongues Untied opens with a series of off-screen chants of "brother to brother, brother to brother." On-screen images of groups of black men move in and out of the camera's frame. The voice-over of an omniscient narrator confesses:

> When talking with a girlfriend, I am more likely to muse about my latest piece or so-and-so's party at Club She-She, than about the anger and hurt I felt that morning when a jeweler refused me entrance to his store because I am Black and male, and we are all perceived as thieves.

The narrator establishes his racial consciousness by remembering his encounter with the racist jeweler. Newsreel footage presents the meeting of a public experience with the personal anger of the narrator. The narrator calls upon his racial brothers to testify as images of black urban uprisings, the destruction of shops, and uniformed police fill the frame in *reel* black and white time. The newsreel footage links the narrator's personal anger with that of his black brothers' very public displays. They take to the streets, as he has taken to the pulpit; they loot and pillage the immediate representatives of capital while he makes a mockery of any black struggle that ignores his very black gay voice. The auditory and visual languages meet where personal and public angers intersect. In an individual instance, the white jeweler refuses the black narrator-subject entry into his store; and in the social instance, white racial convenants refuse the narrator's black community entry into their neighborhoods, schools, and labor unions. The personal is made public.

The film lists individual racist attacks on the body of black men: Howard Beach, Virginia Beach, Yusef Murder, Crack, AIDS; the list constructs a racial and gender community. The signpost question — "Black Men Endangered Species?" — intimates that the answer is Yes. The narrator remains a polyvocal subject since different males speak as its interrogatory voice and the object of its gaze.

A singular image of a nude black man in a sort of death dance dominates the frame. His movements seem to be in response to some impending harm which he wards off. If "black men are an endangered species," then the dancer and warrior have avoided the previous catalogue of death merchants.

Later, the film develops another personal affirmation that involves a dialogue to disrupt homophobia and politically liberate the black gay community. Again, the personal black experience hails a racial and gay-inflected memory that produces oral and visual documents. The musical form of rap provides a venue for a double-voiced, call-and-response testimony. The subconscious reflections of black gay men permeate the communal being and reveal their psychology of homosexual oppression. The narrator, as both *the subject* and *the discourse of the other*, laments:

THE SUBJECT CONFESSES	THE UNCONSCIOUS
Silence is my shield.	(It crushes.)
My cloak.	(It smothers.)
My sword.	(It cuts both ways.)

[THE CONSCIENCE MOVES TOWARDS A
SYNTHESIS OF THE DOUBLED VOICE]

Resistance Appropriates
Silence is the deadliest weapon.
What legacy is to be found in silence?
How many lives lost.
What future lies in our silence?
How much history, lost. So seductive its grip.

This silence . . . Break it.	(Our silence.)
Loose the tongue!	(Testify.)

The double-voiced and double-veiled character of the testimony corresponds with the sociohistorically inflected slave narrative and Jacques Lacan's discussion of "The letter, being and the other." The

Lacanian aspects are generally depicted in the film's articulation and framing of either a gay or a black heterosexual consciousness. Each of the two frames contests the other. It is, however, the testimony that establishes the double-consciousness of the repressed subject. The testimony also awakens the discourse of the OTHER who affirms his black homosexual subjectivity. The dialogic exchange between the veiled-subject and the affirming homosexual Other generates a self-(re)searching discourse that exposes the subject as veiled or closeted while the Other is an emphatic "beyond-the-veil" gay male. Lacan writes, "the unconscious is the discourse of the Other (with a capital O), it is in order to indicate the beyond in which the recognition of desire is bound up with, the desire for recognition."[4]

Similar to the constructive properties of the slave narrative, the film documents an escape which is verified by the presence of male bodies whose names are registered in the film credits. The postNegritude language of *Tongues Untied* negotiates between the conventions accepted by black and gay film audiences and the semidocumentary form. This negotiation is apparent in the film's even-handed affirmation of homosexual and mainstream African American experiences. Interestingly, blacks and gays alternate between negotiation and emphatic resistance by veiled and beyond-the-veiled protest strategies. Marlon Riggs purposely contests homophobia and racism in the black and gay communities. His film bears witness to the double oppression which black gay men encounter.

Tongues Untied documents the formation of a community, which meets at the juncture of race and sexual orientation. The existence of homophobia and racism forces the gay-black subjects to either adopt a twofold reality, or endure racist and/or homophobic attacks. The film successfully depicts a group's coming-into-awareness of an *emphatic* black gay identity. The film creates a black gay narrative tradition to celebrate its socio-historical experience. *Tongues Untied* reaffirms womanist survival strategies, and empowers the slave to resist master narratives that demean both black and gay men alike.

THE PHOTOGRAPHIC FRAMING
OF BLACK MASCULINITY

In a similar manner of double-voiced resistance, Rotimi Fani-Kayode's black male nude photography permits a postNegritude visual identity

Figure 16. "Rotimi Fani-Kayode" by Alex Hirst (© 1988).

that is racial, sexual, and ethnic. He visually creates his subjectivity as politically racial, homosexual, and African. This subsection describes how he negotiates and/or resists the psychological, social, and cultural pressure that would subordinate his black gay subjectivity. My analysis of Rotimi's work explores at least three forms of information. It contrasts Mapplethorpe's photographs of closely framed male genitalia with Rotimi's images of whole black men, not black penises and bottoms. I show how the center of the homoerotic in Mapplethorpe resembles the "Tit and Ass" genre of male heterosexual erotica whereas Rotimi's homoerotic includes the model's torso, face, and limbs. I also discuss the commercial marketing of Mapplethorpe's black homoerotic nudes and how art critics and academic scholars have totally ignored Rotimi's work. Finally, I criticize the complicity of the art houses and the academic taste makers who neglect Rotimi's work and seem enraptured by the fascinating fascism of Mapplethorpe's black male nudes. In "Being Gay: Politics, Identity, Pleasure," Joseph Bristow writes,

> First, gay male identity . . . has always conceived of itself within a sexual politics; that is, within a mutually informing transaction between those two words—a sexualization of politics and a politicization of sex. And second, to be "gay" is not to subscribe to some existential essence. It is instead . . . a strategic identification to express demands in a western world that constantly wants to rid itself of homosexual representation.[5]

Correspondingly, Rotimi's Nigerian gay subjectivity equally invokes a racial politics that resists Eurocentric demands to rid itself of his African retentions. Rotimi's politicization of his black and gay subjectivity is infused with a black dialogic quality. This dialogism is similarly present in the doubly resistant discourses in black womanist art. "Black womanism is a form of resistance to a raceless feminism and a phallocentric pan-Africanism."[6] Rotimi's creativity shares a womanist sensibility and explores, through his use of Yoruba mythology, a multitude of visual assertions of blackness. Each instance of his politicization of race, sexuality, and ethnicity creates a "postNegritude" space that "refers to any moment when members of the black community, through their literature, art, and politics, recognize that black culture is concretely, an open-ended, creative dialogue of subcultures, of insiders and outsiders, of diverse factions."[7]

Robert Mapplethorpe's nude portraits of black males have elicited mixed reactions.[8] Exhibitions of his homoerotic art in federally funded galleries precipitated new limitations on federal appropriations for the arts. Thereafter, each grantee of a National Endowment award must sign affidavits to insure Congress that the monies will not be used to promote, disseminate or produce obscene or indecent materials. My interest, however, is how cultural taste makers have ignored, until recently, the black male nude photography of Rotimi Fani-Kayode, a Nigerian-born and western-educated artist, whose photographs are rarely presented in art galleries outside England. In discussing his work, I first want to indicate how the West and (through their disinterest in black gay art) the Black British and African American communities have permitted Mapplethorpe's black nudes to enjoy an unrivaled place in defining the aesthetics of black male nude photography. Mapplethorpe's photographs of nude black men have had international showings and, as early as 1982, were displayed at the Harlem Exhibition Space, a gallery located in the African American community of Harlem in Manhattan.[9] Ancillary to my analysis is the argument that the critical reception of Mapplethorpe's portraits of black men has authorized Mapplethorpe's black nudes as the first and last statement on black male nude photography in the western world. Second, I will explore the psychological and social tension between bourgeois commonplaces and eruptions of postNegritude funk in the photographic act of revisualizing naked black masculinity. Rotimi's marginal position in black art and his photographic construction of nude black men is one instance of a postNegritude womanist eruption. His mythopoetic images engender a Nigerian homoerotics that disrupts the hegemony of Mapplethorpe's black bodies bent over in anticipation of Western art frames.

One critic's appraisal of Mapplethorpe's Thomas and Dovana[10] finds that the photograph reenacts America's racial fears and fantasies. Ingrid Sischy discusses how it evokes American popularized versions of the master-slave relationship. She writes,

> In 1988 something seems very urgent to me. It has to do with memory, and with freedom. So I chose to emphasize in this essay that part of his work which is a record of our civil battles, and an expression of our civil rights. ... One picture by Mapplethorpe, Thomas and Dovana, epitomizes this. It is of a couple dancing. The man is black; he is naked. The woman is white, she wears a white evening dress, white gloves. She is arched in a melodramatic pose, and he supports her. The picture is a twist, a tie of images that summon Gone With the Wind, Mandingo, and fashion all in one, and the knot that holds it together is very different from anything we might expect. It is opposite of the tradition of burying; it is part of the tradition of showing and thereby knowing.[11]

If Mapplethorpe's vision encompasses the fears and desires of the West, then how do Rotimi's images evoke (or resist) similar fears and desires that are held by the colonial subject? In answering this question, I discuss the postNegritude tension between identifying with authorized marginality (as in Mapplethorpe's work) and empowering a resistant art practice. Rotimi and his artistic practice provide this study with a black gay inflected photographic instance of postNegritude. Implicit in the interpretation of Rotimi's work is the recognition of the uncertain results of the "showing and knowing" creative tradition. Authorial intent never insures against "burying" forms of reception since viewers tend to rely on certain master formulas to decode the unclothed black body. It is the tension between burying the past, discovering its presence, and consciously selecting the appropriate reception formula that creates the critical silence surrounding Rotimi's portraits of black men. Mapplethorpe's black male nudes dramatize racist and (homo)sexual fantasies held by the neocolonial mind. Consequently, his work does little to expose the tension between receptive forms of resistance and negotiation. Since Mapplethorpe's black images are devoid of an ethnic quality, there is no counterpart in Rotimi's Yoruba-inflected black nudes. Significantly, the silence that occasions Rotimi's work manifests the West's primordial erasure of Africa in the history of world art. Similar Western erasures severed the Negroid noses of Egyptian sphinxes.

Rotimi's vision is one example of a postNegritude dilemma in which certain forms of black cultural resistance share visual and psychic space with the colonial discourses on "The Hottentot Venus" and the postcolonial photographic images of "The Hottentot Adonis."

Oluwarotimi Adebiyi Wahab Fani-Kayode was born in Lagos, Nigeria in 1955. His oriki or praise name is: Omo Oliife Abure Omo Ade'de Owo Remo which means child of Ife, child of the crown wealth to the family of the Akire. His family had a traditional spiritual role in Yoruba society. They were keepers of the shrine of Yoruba deities and priests of Ife. The family hails from Ife which is the spiritual center of the Yoruba people.

Politically, Chief Remi Fani-Kayode, Rotimi's father, was leader of the opposition in the Nigerian Parliament in 1960. In four years, he became the Deputy Prime Minister for the Western State, one of three regions of the British colony of Nigeria (Western, Eastern, and Northern). The 1966 military coup ousted Chief Remi Fani-Kayode of his Western State Prime Ministry. The Fani-Kayode family expatriated to England where Rotimi attended primary and secondary school. During this period, Rotimi's father acquired the title of "Balogun of Ife" which is a traditional Yoruba title of "warrior." The position has relevance solely to the Yoruba ethnic group and has little affect on Nigeria's politi-

Figure 17. "Black Boy, Rye" by Alex Hirst (© 1989).

cal administration. Chief Remi Fani-Kayode's two social positions make the Fani-Kayode family an aristocratic, postindependence Nigerian family.

Rotimi lived and attended school in England from 1966 through 1976. Then he traveled to the United States to study at Georgetown University where he received a bachelor's in economics and fine arts in 1980. He attended Pratt Institute in Brooklyn and acquired, in 1983, a master's in fine art and photography. From 1983 until his death in 1989, he lived in London, England. Rotimi's parents financed his undergraduate and graduate education only on condition that their son major in Economics while studying art. During this period, Rotimi began painting and later studied photography. Unlike Robert Mapplethorpe's portraits that focus heavily on black male genitalia,[12] Rotimi's photographs emphasize the centrality of the total black male form and not its physical castrations.

One reason for the art world's ignorance of Rotimi's work is partially due to the artist's decision not to exhibit his photographs in Nigeria or other parts of Africa. Rotimi feared that any African-based presentation of his male nude photography would harm his family's social esteem and lower the political and religious status of the Fani-Kayode patriarch. Rotimi concluded that Nigerians would receive his photographs as a representation of the Fani-Kayode family rather than as his personal vision of black male sexuality:

> As for Africa itself, if I ever manage to get an exhibition in say Lagos, I suspect riots would break out. I would certainly be charged with being a purveyor of corrupt and decadent Western values.
>
> However, sometimes I think that if I took my work into the rural areas, where life is still vigorously in touch with itself and its roots, the reception might be more constructive. Perhaps they would recognise my smallpox Gods, my transsexual priests, my images of desirable Black men in a state of sexual frenzy, or the tranquillity of communion with the spirit world. Perhaps they have far less fear of encountering the darkest of Africa's dark secrets by which some of us seek to gain access to the soul.[13]

He, therefore, never exhibited his nudes in Nigeria. This decision manifests Rotimi's complicity in respecting a status quo that denies his homosexual selfhood as well as its artistic expression. If one considers how problematic it is for a gay Nigerian to inherit the title of the "Balogun of Ife," then one arrives at the postNegritude moment when patriarchal and heterosexist traditions collide with recognition that the rightful heir to the title "Balogun of Ife" is a homosexual photographer.

Resistance is a complex and slippery action that sociopsychical and economic hegemonies most often nullify. Illustratively, Rotimi

 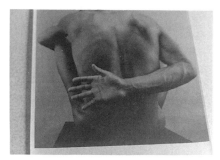

Figure 18. Seeing No Evil In Self-Blindness.   **Figure 19.** Turning Away From Reality.

complied with the hegemonies of heterosexism and Yoruba tradition and, thereby, denied his sexuality to his Nigerian public while he explored it under the agency of Western art photography. His decision exemplifies a postNegritude process of "double talk," a process laden with contradictions and gaps in consciousness.

While enrolled at Pratt Institute, Rotimi worked in the costly processing medium of color photography. As long as his parents financed his education he continued to work with color photography and developed a photographic style that employs Yoruba folk images. For example, Rotimi's early photographic work is characterized by surrealistic color portraits of black men in Yoruba attire. Alex Hirst, a British photographer-filmmaker and cofounder of the art journal *Square Peg*, says Rotimi's imagery "came out of his African experience and his physical separation from Africa. His work is more influenced by Africa than by his experience in the West. Rotimi felt that he had been cheated of his Yoruba culture since he, along with his family, was forced into political exile."[14]

Rotimi, like other doubly exiled artists, must reconcile the fact of separation by narrating that rupture. Rotimi says of his ruptures, "On three counts I am an outsider: in matters of sexuality; in terms of geographical and cultural dislocation; and in the sense of not having become the sort of respectably married professional my parents might have hoped for."[15] Rotimi uses a confessional narrative style that is visualized in his nude photographs of black men. Each photograph expresses his attempts to reconcile the first two of the three forms of exile that he mentioned—that of his Yoruba self from Nigeria and that of his black-gay self from an expatriate Nigerian community in England. Rotimi is an expatriate Nigerian who yearns for his cultural past but who is further marginalized by a past that refuses his gay presence. Only in a postNegritude moment is one confronted with the question, can a homosexual inherit the Yoruba title of Balogun warrior? Rotimi's photographs permit a sort of imaginary memory in which his gay identity converges within contested spaces of postindependent Africa which has politically and psychologically suffered fragmentation.

Instances similar to Rotimi's predicament force Africans and African diasporic people to reassess their past and reformulate the constitutional elements of blackness. Critic Teshome H. Gabriel finds that "Our memory is always subject to change depending on several factors. To some, memory is an impediment, something to be forgotten. But the power of memory is such that in struggling to forget . . . one (is) in fact reinforcing the very power to recall."[16]

Psychologically speaking, Rotimi's decision to show his male nudes exclusively in Western metropolises (for example, New York and London) is an act of both self-denial and self-affirmation. He denies his homoerotic art in Africa but celebrates it in countries where both his black and gay identities make him doubly an outcast. He is similar to African American and Afro-Caribbean expatriates (such as Josephine Baker, Sidney Bechet, Richard Wright, Chester Himes, and Frantz Fanon), since he and previous black expatriates discover and recreate their racial identity through fictive memories which paradoxically desire recognition in western capitals and cultural marketplaces.

Because Rotimi's work escapes recognition in Nigeria, his photographs are, then, living spirits in search of their Yoruba roots—imagined and real. Rotimi's nude images dramatize the uncertainty of where Nigeria ends and his exiled, Western self begins. It is not Rotimi's fault that his photographs are incomplete fragments warring for some sense of wholeness in which a diasporic Yoruba culture celebrates and affirms black male sexuality in all its forms. He and his resistance are determined by a postNegritude dilemma in which Blacks bury certain elements of their oppression while they reaffirm other aspects. Rotimi's photographs alter traditional Yoruba perceptions about the inheritor of the Balogun title as well as the sociopolitical and familial image of the Nigerian Deputy Prime Minister of the Western Province.

A narrow interpretation of Rotimi's photographs would reduce his work and vision to a singular African or Yoruba or gay aesthetic. His

Figure 20. White Hands Over Black Man's Eyes.

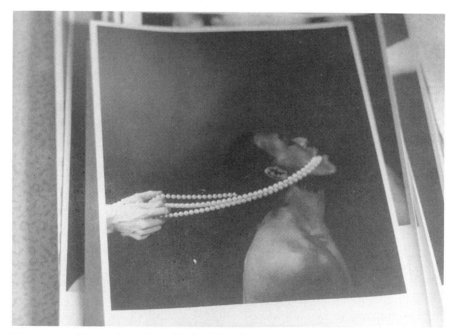

Figure 21. The Pearls and Perils of Colonialism.

photography, however, presents one of many forms of black male sexuality and articulates a dialogic tension between racial, ethnic, and sexual affirmations as well as the discourses that deny such utterances of racial, ethnic, and sexual pride. One must recognize that the colonial experience mutually affects the social and psychic constitution of the West.

Consequently, Rotimi's photographs are embedded with an erotic blackness that speaks to both Africa and the West. His images question the dehumanizing gaze-narratives that objectified the black body as unruly and warranting excisions. The excessive dismembering of the black body is evident in the extreme close-ups of black penises on display in both Robert Mapplethorpe's *Black Book* and Leni Riefenstahl's *The Last of the Nuba*.[17] In commenting on Riefenstahl's ethnographic photography, Rotimi reminds us that

> Some Western photographers have shown that they can desire Black males (albeit rather neurotically). But the exploitative mythologising of Black virility on behalf of the homosexual bourgeoisie is ultimately no different from the vulgar objectification of Africa which we know at one extreme from the work of Leni Riefenstahl and, at the other from the "victim" images which appear constantly in the media.[18]

The images in these books reveal racial fantasies masked by acceptable anthropological and fine art formulae. The works bury the social history of racial lynching and castrations which they indirectly recast in socially acceptable forms. Frantz Fanon interprets this western fantasy in a similar manner:

> The white man is convinced that the Negro is a beast; if it is not the length of the penis, then it is the sexual potency that impresses him. Face to face with this man who is "different from himself," he needs to defend himself. In other words, to personify The Other. The Other will become the mainstay of his preoccupations and his desires.[19]

Correspondingly, the genitalia of the black female have equally been objectified in modernist art such as in Pablo Picasso's Olympia (1901), on the Parisian cabaret stage in Josephine Baker's "banana dance" (c. 1926–1927),[20] and in the nineteenth century's "scientific" excisions of the "Hottentot Venus." The history of the Hottentot Venus reveals how a colonial speculum (a mirrored viewing posture of scientific pretensions) physically and psychologically separates the genitalia of African women from those of their western equivalents—Victorian ladies (here, the size of the black vagina and, correspondingly, the black penis are used as pseudoscientific facts to exclude black sexuality from the civilized world. The language reduces Blacks to a primitive image and an unrestrained sexuality). Sander Gilman describes the scientific discourse of the day as found in the work of J. D. Virey, whom he describes as

> The author of the study of race standard in the early nineteenth century and also contributed a major essay (the only one on a specific racial group) to the widely cited Dictionnaire des sciences medicales . . . (1819). In this essay, Virey summarized his (and his contemporaries') views on the sexual nature of black females in terms of acceptable medical discourse. According to him, their "voluptuousness" is "developed to a degree of lascivity unknown in our climate, for their sexual organs are much more developed than those of whites."[21]

Just as Mapplethorpe uses art photography and Rotimi appropriates Yoruba and Western art conventions, Virey appropriates an "acceptable" form by extrapolating his extrascientific discourse on the psychology of black females from the physiognomy of their sexual organs. When Mapplethorpe selectively frames well-endowed black glans, his photographs visualize a "Hottentot Adonis" and refer to the "voluptuousness" discourse of Virey. One could also plausibly read Mapplethorpe's black men as a critical reflection of such racial fantasies in the minds of Western (wo)mankind.

Melody D. Davis, an art critic, in commenting on Mapplethorpe's photograph of George Bradshaw's backside,[22] finds that "Mapplethorpe idealized blacks in negation of the personal, the social, and, even, the function of gender."[23] In describing Mapplethorpe's psychological impulse, Davis quotes from the writing of psychologist Janine Chasseguet-Smirgel who finds that "Idealization conceals but changes nothing."[24] Davis adds, "George Bradshaw (1980) relates to anality, control, and sadism. . . . with his glamorized buttocks, [he] signals the forbidden and the desired—man as mother. This [black] one, however, is possessable. For Mapplethorpe, who seldom fetishized whites in the purely objectifying manner he had toward blacks, racial difference substituted for that of gender."[25]

Rotimi's work, on the other hand, is not as ambiguous in intent yet it may also enliven Virey's colonial discourse on "the Hottentot woman (and by implication the Hottentot man) as the epitome of this sexual lasciviousness [which] stresses the relation between . . . physiology and . . . physiognomy." If the Hottentot woman is expressed in this light then the Hottentot man and his genitalia, physiology, and physiognomy express an equal degree of sexual lasciviousness. Oddly and tellingly, the speculum, a mirror instrument, was used to expose the interior cavities of the various black women who were collectively called "the Hottentot Venus."[26] Nevertheless, the nude images in the works of both Mapplethorpe and Rotimi also mirror the interior psychic workings of Western society and provide different frames for the Hottentot Adonis.

Rotimi's nudes distance the colonialist gaze and Mapplethorpe's white suburban fantasies. True, Rotimi's photographs do not escape the already-existing Hottentot histories of primitive black sexuality or avoid his Nigerian past. The artist and his art are born into a history that determines how others perceive his work. Yet Rotimi acknowledges the force of Western history and his ability to rediscover and revalidate his Yoruba past:

> The history of Africa and of the Black race has been constantly distorted. Even in Africa, my education was given in English in Christian schools, as though the language and culture of my own people, the Yoruba, were inadequate or in some way unsuitable. . . . In exploring Yoruba history and civilization, I have rediscovered and revalidated areas of my experience and understanding of the world. I see parallels now between my own work and that of the Osogbo artists in Yorubaland who themselves have resisted the cultural subversions of neo-colonialism and who celebrate the rich, secret world of our ancestors.[27]

His photographs celebrate a complex black body that has been bombarded by past excisions. Rotimi articulates this in saying, "It is now time for us to reappropriate such images and to transform them ritualistically into images of our own creation. For me, this involves an imaginative investigation of Blackness, maleness and sexuality, rather than more straightforward reportage."[28] In his reappropriation of "accept-able" master discourses, he exorcises colonial fantasies through the creation of alternative myths.

Theoretical discourses on postcolonial/postNegritude subjectivity must acknowledge that the continuation of the Civil Rights movement and the development of a multiracial feminism require the recognition of multiple subject positions that embrace fissures, gaps, and cyclical setbacks. This realization enables intermittent spaces to reconstitute self and society. It permits irreverent eruptions, like Rotimi's photographs, to represent and interpret the rich interstices of race, ethnicity, gender, and sexuality which are all parts of black subjectivity.

In reading Rotimi's photographs, one must pursue a cultural criticism that articulates gaps and fissures. This form of open-ended readings permits free zones of discourse and denies monolithic and hegemonic closures that create binaries of us versus them, east versus west, gay versus straight, and black versus white. As Trinh T. Minh-Ha asserts, "No system functions in isolation. No First World exists independently from the Third World; there is a Third World in every First World and vice-versa."[29] Additionally, this denial of systemic closure tends to reject critical theories which complacently accept the inevitability of a demoralized and overdetermined socioeconomic present as the singular effect of postmodernity when the postmodern also encompasses "a social category—a dominant yet diverse set of structural and institutional processes wherein certain sensibilities, styles, and outlooks are understood as reactions and responses to new societal conditions and historical circumstances."[30] One can neither deny the heterogeneity of psychic forms of reception nor romantically ignore that sociohistorical experiences overdetermine the receptive processes of encoding and decoding naked black images.

The refusal of one London art gallery to show Rotimi's work because, according to these managers of British culture, his work merely imitated Mapplethorpe's, reflects the overdetermined nature of hegemonic modes of reception. Equally overdetermined (in a very colonialist way) is the view held by certain blacks that Rotimi's photographs represent European decadence. Contrary to Mapplethorpe's work which speaks to and denies European colonial fantasies, Rotimi Fani-Kayode's work as well as his social predicament is an eruption of postNegritude funk. Rotimi, the inheritor of the Balogun of Ife title, lived in Nigeria, London, Washington D.C., and New York. Mapplethorpe's experience was confined to his Catholic, suburbanite upbringing and his encounters with a multicultural, gay Manhattan.

Rotimi was aware of Western art and the fetishization of certain aspects of the black body. But his black males are framed as complete bodies which are sometimes adorned with Nigerian significance, as in his portrait of a nude black male holding a large fish.

Here, Rotimi presents a homoerotic portrait of a Nigerian fisherman without his briefs.[31] Although Rotimi and Mapplethorpe are both gay photographers who explore black male sexuality, Rotimi is not obsessed with close-ups of well-endowed black glans. He resists Mapplethorpe's vacillating vision of the black male as, depending on one's reading of his work, (un)threatening and (un)worthy of artistic and judicial beheading in all its legal and extralegal forms. (One need only to view Mapplethorpe's zipper-castration of the black "Man in Polyester Suit"[32] to appreciate this point). Rotimi deemphasizes the very parts of the black body that Mapplethorpe and other white males have scientifically scrutinized, legally censored, and erased in lynching.

Stuart Hall finds that:

> Mapplethorpe's handling of the black male figure is always hovering on the brink of voyeurism (when it is not actually collapsing into it) and his truncation of the black body always amplifies its fetishistic effect, objectifying black sexuality. Fani-Kayode "subjectifies" the black male, and black sexuality, claiming it, without making it an object of contemplation and at the same time without "personifying it."[33]

I want to acknowledge that Mapplethorpe's vision is not reflective of his individual agency but of a cultural and social experience which includes encounters with black and white men. As expressed earlier, the master's discourse is mutually shared by the colonizer and the colonized.

In a 1986 article entitled "True Confessions," and in its 1991 revised form, "Looking For Trouble," Kobena Mercer notes that certain black gays are titillated by Mapplethorpe's fetishistic images of black men, and that therefore black gay reception is hailed by a colonial fantasy. According to Mercer, the photographs

> encourage the viewer to examine his or her own implication in the fantasies that the images arouse. Once I acknowledge my own implication in the image reservoir as a gay subject, as

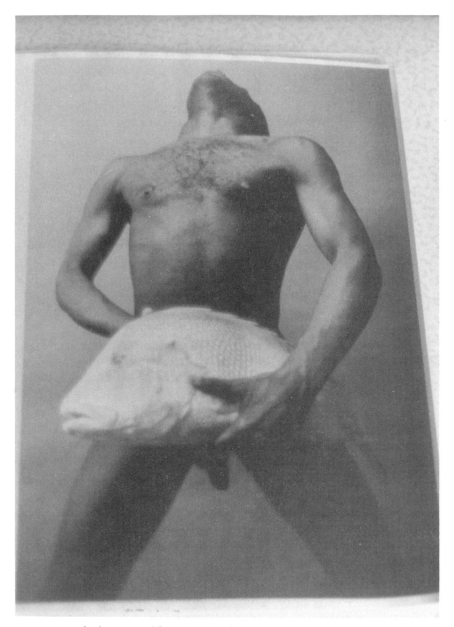

Figure 22. Black Man Holding Large Fish.

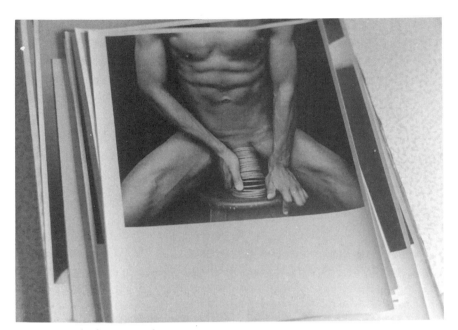

Figure 23. Black Man With Wire.

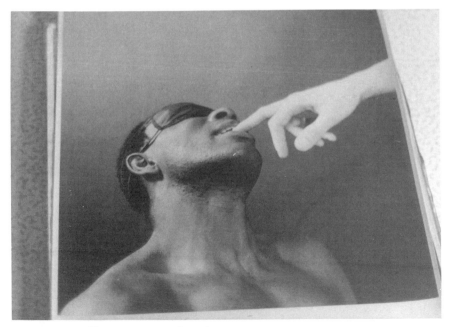

Figure 24. Suckling A Dying Colonialism.

a desiring subject for whom the aestheticized object of the look represents an object choice already there in my own fantasies, then I am forced to confront the unwelcome fact that as a spectator I actually inhabit the same position in fantasy of mastery which I said earlier was that of the hegemonic white male subject![34]

In addition, Mercer discovers a sort of liberal humanistic function in Mapplethorpe's use of the nude black body within the context of Western art history. Having retracted his previous critique of Mapplethorpe's objectification of black men and black sexuality as a product of white male hegemony, he writes,

> Previously, I argued that the fixative function of the stereotype played the decisive role in reproducing colonial fantasy: now, however, in relation to Mapplethorpe's authorial identity as an explicitly gay artist (located, like other gay artists, on the margins of mainstream art-world institutions), it becomes possible, and necessary, to reverse that view and recognize the way in which his aesthetic strategy begins to subvert the hierarchy of the cultural codes that separate the pure and noble values of the fine art nude from the filthy and degraded form of the commonplace racist stereotype.[35]

Mercer's reassessment of Mapplethorpe permits him to allude to the symbiotic relationship between fine art and ordinary racism. In a similar vein, I want to reassess how the surplus of critical attention accorded to Mapplethorpe's aesthetic strategy of subverting Western fine art promotes the deficit of critical attention directed at Rotimi's aesthetic strategy. Surely, Rotimi's camera eye subverts the hierarchy of the cultural codes that separate the pure and noble values of the fine art nude from commonplace racism? But Rotimi's work avoids the shortcomings that Stuart Hall finds in the subversive strategy of Mapplethorpe. Hall views Mapplethorpe's work as "hovering on the brink of voyeurism (when it is not actually collapsing into it)" and holds that "his truncation of the black body always amplifies its fetishistic effect, objectifying black sexuality."

In the 1986 version of the article, which appears in a British journal, Kobena Mercer and Isaac Julien observe that

> Mapplethorpe appropriates the conventions of porn's racialised codes of representation and by abstracting its stereotypes into

"art" he makes racism's phantasms of desire respectable. . . . In pictures like "Man in a Polyester Suit," the dialectics of fear and fascination in colonial fantasy are reinscribed by the centrality of the black man's 'monstrous' phallus. The black subject is objectified into Otherness as the size of his penis symbolises a threat to the secure identity of the white male ego.[36]

During the same year Mercer wrote "Imagining the Black Man's Sex" which was published in a 1987 British critical anthology on photography. He borrows Michel Foucault's essay "What is an Author" to discuss the overdetermined nature of hegemonic forms of reception. He correctly argues that Mapplethorpe's black nudes reflect the sociopsychic image of black male sexuality regardless of the racial, sexual, and gender identity of the viewer. Mercer writes that the male nudes

> facilitate the public projection of certain sexual and racial fantasies about the black male body. Whatever his creative pretensions or psychological motivations, Mapplethorpe's camera-eye opens an aperture onto aspects of stereotypes—a fixed way of seeing that freezes the flux of experience—of black men which circulate in pornography . . . and other systems of representation.[37]

In returning to his most recent Mapplethorpe study, "Looking For Trouble," one discovers the surplus that a capitalistic system creates when objects are in high demand. The critic and the system of academic publishing permit the recirculation of an insightful reflection and, paradoxically, reveal the complicity of leftist criticism in this capitalistic process.

Unfortunately—and not to dismiss the importance of Mercer's analysis—the essay and its recycled forms do little to reveal how black male (heterosexual and gay) artists are disempowered by the popularity and currency of critical essays about Mapplethorpe's black men. Is it possible to redirect this surplus of critical attention to this white artist's reflection of colonial desires and fears? How have certain academics and art critics participated in their own erasure while situating themselves in neocolonialist double-talking positions?

On another interpretive level, one might analyze how Mercer's revisions reveal the overdetermined nature of academic discourses that focus on such Eurocentric frames as Mapplethorpe's gay vision of black men (who cannot be photographed as essentially gay or heterosexual)?

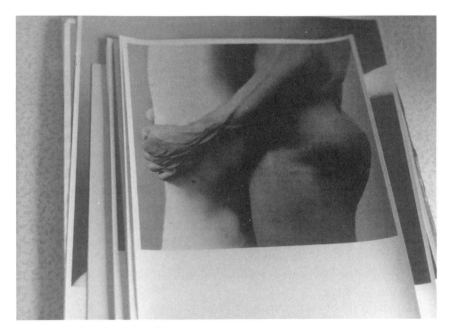

Figure 25. The Chaotic Embrace.

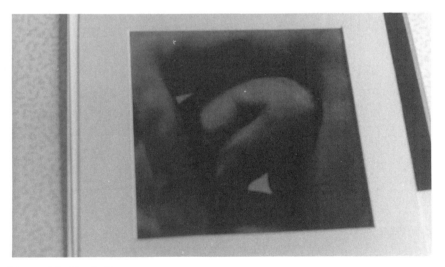

Figure 26. The In-Betweenness.

Are progressive academics not equally guilty (I still share some of this guilt) in the circulation of colonial fantasy when they limit their readings to the colonizer's products, rather than interpreting the oppositional fantasies of the colonized?

I implicitly support Mercer's use of Foucault to emphasize the shared nature of colonial readings and the Bakhtinian notion of heteroglossia as multiple forms of reception which permit alternative readings. Mercer understands this in-between aspect of image reception:

> Although they reproduce the syntax of common-sense racism, the inscribed or preferred meanings of these images are not fixed; they can, at times, be prised apart into alternative readings when different experiences are brought to bear on their interpretation. . . . black readers may reappropriate pleasures which over-turn signs of otherness into signs of identity.[38]

I, however, find it more effective to analyze the dilemma facing a black gay photographer whose nude portraits do not enjoy the surplus of attention that welcomes Mapplethorpe's black nudes. Syntactically, Rotimi Fani-Kayode's male nudes rarely if ever reflect a visual complicity with colonial fantasies. Yet, Rotimi's intentions cannot avoid receptions that psychologically reappropriate his reappropriation to generate a return to the initial primitive and lusty forms of reception.

There exist no guarantees that Rotimi's work is or ever will be solely appreciated by connoisseurs and collectors of gay art. Though he works mostly with black gay models, Rotimi's nudes are not essentially an articulation of a blackened homoerotic desire. His photographs speak to panAfrican interests in Yoruba folk culture. They celebrate the black body as human and whole. They reflect a multivocal discourse of postNegritude and, in a Bakhtinian sense, a translinguistic eroticism which, as Robert Stam describes,

> would speak of sexual heteroglossia, i.e., the many-languagedness of sexual pleasure and practice, what Helene Cixous calls the "thousands of tongues" of eroticism. An erotic translinguistics would look for "dialogism" on every level—interpersonal, intra-textual, intertextual, interspectatorial—and combat an array of monologisms—the monologism of patriarchy, of heterosexism, or Puritanism. Its emphasis would be

not on unilateral desire but rather on what Bakhtin would call the "in-between" of erotic locution.[39]

Rotimi provides an African place inbetween the classical Greek nude and the African warrior. He leaves his multiracial, sexual, gender, and ethnic audience with an imaginative, illusive, and slippery sensuality that frames his nudes. Such slippery and illusive qualities are not always available to artists who, like Mapplethorpe, attempt to deal with the epic narrative of black sexuality by showing it in the colonial speculum of racist frames. While Mapplethorpe's black nudes focus on the phallic threat of black manhood as erotic and dangerous to the Western mind,[40] Fani-Kayode's black nudes emphasize the humanity of the total black body as sensual and significant.

5

BLACK WOMEN AND
INTERRACIAL LOVE

I n previous chapters, I explained postNegritude as a philosophical, theoretical, and activist paradigm that arose from such socio-psychical movements as the civil rights, women's, and gay liberation movements of the late sixties through the Reagan-Bush eighties. To-gether, these sociopsychical and activist movements helped to produce a different form of black art for a more racially diverse audience than was the case before black women secured a position in the market places of culture and commerce. One needs only cite the Nobel Prize-winning author Toni Morrison, the television producer and talk-show hostess Oprah Winfrey, the U.S. Senator Carol Mosely-Braun, and most recently, Anita Hill. Before these women achieved their respective mainstream successes, womanist ideals confronted the various narrative modes of masculinist production.

I also examined how postNegritude and womanist creativity and political activism intervene in the visual and literary arts. These inter-ventions disrupt the everyday racist, masculinist, and homophobic ide-ologies and effect change by offering alternatives to reductionist think-ing. The first chapter discussed how postNegritude is an inclusive type of Negritude that does not valorize any one type of black experience because it acknowledges multiple forms of blackness. This attitude has guided my analysis of visual and literary works and commits my analysis to showing real alternatives to deterministic patterns of personal, social, and sexual being of blackness.

LOVE THAT DARE NOT SEEK
ITS REPRESENTATION

This chapter returns postNegritude analysis to the cinematic construction of interracial and multiracial forms of black intimacy. Discussion will indicate how particular filmmakers construct interracial heterosexual intimacy between black women and nonblack men. The earlier chapters discussed the production of black art by black diasporic people; I now traverse the racial boundaries of black artistic production to study how a few representative post-eighties films portray interracial intimacy between black women and white men.

The representative films that I focus on feature a black actress who stars as the lover of a major white male character. The black female must be desired by, and equally desirous of, the white male. Even though the topic of interracial intimacy between black men and nonblack women is not of central importance, I will also refer to a few films treating this issue and compare the various ways this topic is dramatized in contemporary films written and/or directed by such black filmmakers as Spike Lee.

My analysis will not provide an encyclopedic list of all films that dramatize this particular type of interracial intimacy. I choose, however, to describe how one recent film depicts a young black heroine who is romantically involved with an equally young white man. In my description and analysis, I hold that postNegritude identity has always existed alongside dominant movements from the 1950s through the 1980s. PostNegritude identity and its construction have recently appeared in a few films (including *Jungle Fever*, with Spike Lee's depiction of Orin Goode and Paulie Carbone) that treat a *sustainable* form of interracial intimacy between black women and white men.

I have chosen to analyze this particular type of interracial romance because of the paucity of writing on the cinematic representation of black women in romantic relationships with white men. Most discussions that broach the topic of transracial unions are interested in black men—patriarchy, and white women—the possessions of white patriarchs. Films also usually depict transracial unions as uniquely black male and white female; they thereby create monolithic forms of such transracial unions. Granted, patriarchy and racist conventions have assisted in this lack of production, but it is also a result of the lack of importance given to this subgenre in general by film scholars and other critics of popular culture. Correspondingly, even the study of films depicting black men in intimate unions with white women does not have a long history. A list of films that seriously treat this theme would have just a few titles including Larry Peerce's *One Potato, Two Potato* (1964), Herbert Danska's *Sweet Love Bitter* (1966), and Melvin Van Peebles' *Story of a Three-Day Pass* (1967). Even fewer films exist that deal with black heroines romantically involved with white males. Here, we must deal with "who's passing for whom" and "the tragic mulatta" master discourse which determined many Hollywood films before the sixties.

Surely, there exist pre-1960s films that depict intimacy between black females and white males, but either such depictions are not central to the narrative, or a white actress performs the black heroine's role and the major theme concerns her racial passing not interracial love. Such films as *Pinky* (1949), *Kings Go Forth* (1958), *Imitation of Life* (1959), and *Night of the Quarter Moon* (1959) feature white actresses acting the role of a black heroine who dates and/or marries the white male lead. Hollywood studios, even after the demise of the sacrosanct Hays Code that forbade the depiction of interracial love, honored this convention. In the mind of mainstream America, the object of a white man's love must be a white woman. Jeanne Crain, Natalie Wood, Susan Kohner, and Julie London, respectively, performed a mainstream function similar to that of their fifties contemporary Elvis Presley. Elvis was a talented white rebel who moved his pelvis in a way that psychologically evoked the sexually potent image of his black male Others—Chuck Berry and Little Richard.

These pre-'60s types of melodramas feature at least three forms of racial negations. First, studios avoid casting black actresses as the heroine. Second, the white actress cast as the black heroine creates a cycle of films featuring white women in black interracial romances. Lastly, the narrative never truly disrupts the psychosocial taboo against white men romantically attracted to and marrying black women. It is quite telling that there are few if any post-World War II films which treat interracial romance and feature black actresses in roles as white heroines who are romantically involved with white male characters. This absence reflects the unyielding convention against cinematically treating romantic, as opposed to lustful, relationships between black women and white men.

Some readers may find that this absence should be celebrated, while others want to know how a recent film depicts black women (as opposed to white women in blackface) in *lasting* interracial unions that are not built on lusty desires. Here "lasting" means that the relationship

Figure 27. Pinky (Jeanne Crain) and her grandmother (Ethel Waters) in *Pinky.*

endures the narrative closures of break-ups, divorce, and the death of one of the two lovers. The word "lusty" does not infer a moral judgment; it merely helps to describe romance which, unlike lust, is not totally a function of one's libido.

ALLIANCES WITH DAYDREAMING BELIEVERS

The integrationist-assimilationist period offered little change in the depiction of black women loving white men. Nevertheless, the period's sociocultural and political changes did prepare a new generation of moviegoers for this reality. Film audiences became more open to stories that challenged their outlook on interracial romance. However, most moviegoers sought, and were given, closure to these affairs before the film concluded.

The civil-rights movement spans more than fifty years of interracial alliances between black and white Americans. In attempting to explain its demise since the seventies, popular explanations describe it as resulting from the growing rift between African American and Jewish Communities. For instance, Cornel West explains,

> The period of genuine empathy and principled alliances between Jews and [B]lacks (1910–67) constitutes a major pillar of American progressive politics in this century. These supportive links begin with W.E.B. Du Bois's *The Crisis* and Abraham Cahan's *Jewish Daily Forward* and are seen clearly between Jewish leftists and A. Philip Randolph's numerous organizations, between Elliot Cohen's *Commentary* and the early career of James Baldwin, between prophets like Abraham Joshua Heschel and Martin Luther King, Jr.[1]

I, however, understand white American progressives as a more inclusive group that transcends any one particular religious group and its culture. Given this understanding, any interracially sponsored civil rights agenda had whites who were Jewish and others who were as Christian and Catholic as Dorothy Day, the cofounder of the *Catholic Worker*. Surely, it was a general movement in which disparate groups discovered their dissimilar but equally dehumanizing trajectories of oppression. This broader understanding of the progressive movement helps to explain why civil-rights legislation and affirmative action now safeguard women, the elderly, the handicapped and, in certain regions, homosexuals.

The liberal-integrationist alliances were also apparent in the art community and in certain levels of the film industry. For example, the Beat movement attracted various ethnic groups; a few African Americans such as Bob Kaufman and LeRoi Jones were major players. When LeRoi Jones became Amiri Baraka it marked a break with Allen Ginsberg and other Beat writers including black Bob Kaufman, Italian American Lawrence Ferlinghetti, and Baraka's white Jewish wife Hettie Jones. This break was also with other black intellectuals and artists of this period, including Hansberry and Walker, who formed lasting friendships and even married outside their race. In the film industry, the liberal transracial alliance was visually popularized in such Sidney Poitier vehicles such as *No Way Out* (1950), *The Defiant Ones* (1958), *A Patch of Blue* (1965), *To Sir With Love* (1967), and *Guess Who's Coming to Dinner* (1967).

By the end of the sixties, America's general political climate can be characterized as a "shoot to kill," rather than maim, conservatism.

Figure 28. Richard Widmark, Linda Darnell, and Sidney Poitier in *No Way Out.*

Given the general political climate and urban unrest, Malcolm X and Dr. King's murders were harbingers to the end of this cycle of integrationist films. Again, I should indicate that by the end of this historical moment interracial sentiment was anything but acceptable to the Black Arts movement as has been demonstrated in my discussion of the John A. Williams novel, *The Man Who Cried I Am* (1967) and is evident in Amiri Baraka's seminal plays *Dutchman* (1964) and *The Slave* (1964).

Culture wars over inclusion in the "Canon" and economic wars over affirmative action—the war for inclusion in America's work places—followed. These civil wars over culture and economics further damaged America's race relations. Black nationalist sentiments, as mentioned in earlier chapters, became potent psychological tools that were used by many African American artists from the late sixties through the early eighties. The alliance between America's black and white liberals was now threatened. Their cheery vision of a race-blind America had increasingly become bruised and offensive to the economically disenfranchised black community. Their hopes seemed to be merely hallucinatory fantasy featured in Poitier vehicles and 1949 problem films. In the eighties, a few films reworked Poitier's integrationist heroics by using white men and a variety of nonwhite women portraying interracial intimacies. Black actresses acquired major roles as women in intimate relations with white male characters. These films offered black actresses and black female characterizations a very different image than offered by white actresses in blackface impersonating a simulation of black womanhood. The psychological needs of postwar America who viewed and identified with *Pinky, Kings Go Forth, Imitation of Life,* and *Night of the Quarter Moon* now had to deal with nothing but the "real" thing.

Using a comparative approach, I shall examine how these fiction films slyly recycle integrationist politics and Black-Jewish alliances through the agency of interracial intimacy. My reading of these films will also note how the narrative accommodates, negotiates, or resists societal pressures that would thwart interracial intimacy, Black-Jewish alliances, and black female subjectivity.

Earlier, I mentioned a list of films that explore this subject but rarely dramatize enduring unions between black women and white men. Of those that do, there is, for instance, Spike Lee's *Jungle Fever,* where the burgeoning friendship between the Italian American Paulie Carbone and the African American Orin Goode might endure. Similarly but more developed, Julie Dash's *Daughters of the Dust* features an interracial union between Iona Peazant and St. Julian Last Child, a Cherokee. In black theater, there is Adrienne Kennedy's absurdist play *Funnyhouse of a Negro* which depicts a tormented interracial union between mixed-race "Sarah, the Negro" and Raymond, her Jewish American lover. Recent filmmakers, including Lee and Dash, have moderately focused on the black female character in interracial unions, and made important inroads in the visual depiction of this transracial experience.

IN THE MAINSTREAM OF POSTNEGRITUDE TIMES

Popular contemporary action films, like *The Bodyguard* (1992) and *Deep Cover* (1992), dramatically deemphasize the sociocultural differences between the black heroine and her white lover. In the case of *The Bodyguard,* the heroine's sociocultural identity is as rhythmically flat as Whitney Houston singing the American national anthem. In *Deep Cover,* the interracial relationship is of minor importance to the development of the crime plot. Popular contemporary comedies, on the other hand, tend to efface the heroine's black sociocultural identity in a much different way. Comedies like *White Men Can't Jump* (1992) and *Made In America* (1993), comically exaggerate the sociocultural differences. Thus, moviegoers watch Whoopi Goldberg performing one of her self-demeaning comic skits and Rosie Perez performing a streetwise oversexed but lovable Afro-Latina. In these films, neither the black heroine nor the interracial union is of much substance. The films develop a masquerade of transgressive love that is no more, and no less, threatening to the general moviegoer than the postwar cycle of films that featured white women in blackface—*Pinky, Kings Go Forth, Imitation of Life*, and *Night of the Quarter Moon*. With one brush stroke, these films paint interracial landscapes in varying racial tones; with another brush stroke, they hide cultural differences behind the pale mask of white actresses. Such films permit the white mate and mainstream taste to consume the black heroine's corporal image without transgressing dominant racial conventions. Yes, I admit that black actresses sometimes give great performances in these roles. But this success may work to limit their talents to such roles. This is the case with Whoopi Goldberg and Rosie Perez. I also agree that we should celebrate these actresses, and the industry, because they have finally received major roles. Nonetheless, I still look forward to a time when studios cast black actresses in roles that equal their talents. This has rarely been the case for Whoopi Goldberg and Rosie Perez.

In addition to the Goldberg and Perez interracial vehicles, the nineties introduced younger black actresses in affairs with equally young white men. Many of these films confront racist and misogynist myths in new and interesting ways. The importance of the black heroine's racial and cultural difference is alluded to without constructing these differences in sexually exaggerated and racially demeaning images. This group of films also shows that individuals of the same economic class, regardless of their racial and national differences, share similar romantic and philosophical interests. John Duigan's *Flirting* (1991) depicts interracial love between teenagers in a rural Australian boarding school in 1965. It features two teenagers who are from different races, nations, and class backgrounds, but the glue that holds them together is their vision of a society where they do not have to honor thoughtless social conventions. Of all the recent films that depict this form of interracial intimacy, this film presents an original take on the coming-of-age film genre in that the young black heroine is intelligent, sensitive, sensual and cosmopolitan. Similarly, the young white hero is intelligent, sensitive, and sensual but not as urbane as the heroine. Usually, the interracial romance subgenre rarely features this type of transracial union of *equals*. Analysis will ascertain how the film resists reductive racist, nationalist, and sexist ideologies that would appear to end the relationship. A large part of the analysis discerns how accommodation, negotiation, and resistance liberate the two from societal pressures. There are several other films that feature black women with white men but my purpose here has never been to create an encyclopedic list. It is more effective to focus on a specific instance and then express a general opinion about the contemporary and historical importance of this type of film.

FLIRTING: BORDER CROSSINGS OF RACE AND NATION

John Duigan wrote and directed *The Year My Voice Broke* (1987) which tells of the coming-of-age of Danny Embling (Noah Taylor) in a rural Australian town in 1962. In 1991, Duigan directed *Flirting*, a sequel to *The Year My Voice Broke*. The story is set in 1965 at St. Albans Boys School in rural Australia. Danny, reluctantly, attends St. Albans where he is bullied by his more athletic school chums. Opposite St. Albans and across the lake is Cirencester Ladies College which Thandiwe Adjewa, his soon-to-be girlfriend, attends.

Thandiwe is a Ugandan of mixed-racial parentage. Her deceased mother's parents were white English and black Kenyan. Thandiwe's father is a world-renowned Ugandan intellectual who has a one-year lectureship at the University of Canberra. The death of her mother during the Mau Mau period in Kenya, her father's nationalist writings and lectures, and her international encounters with other intellectuals have helped shape her interest in world affairs. Thandiwe's racial identity, international concerns, and her love for Danny create tensions for both her and Danny. The tensions are neither as serious nor as debilitating as presented in the films *Pinky* and *Jungle Fever* and the literary works *The Man Who Cried I Am* and *The Funnyhouse of a Negro*. Neither Thandiwe nor Danny suffers the physical and unending psychological abuses that welcome the interracial couples in previously discussed works. Similar to the Orin Goode-Paulie Carbone relationship in *Jungle Fever*, *Flirting*'s narrative closure on interracial teenage

Figure 29. Melissa Miles (Kym Wilson), Thandiwe Adjewa (Thandie Newton), Danny Embling (Noah Taylor), Janet Odgers (Naomi Watts), and "Gilby" Fryer (Bartholomew Rose) in a scene from *Flirting.*

love does not guarantee a definitive end. The film ends as Thandiwe returns to Uganda where her father has been imprisoned after his return to the country. Just as her English-Kenyan mother had died during Kenya's Mau Mau, now, her Ugandan writer-father and her stepmother will also meet a similar death. Thandiwe Adjewa is far from the stereotypical image of Africans and young black women. Her presence in this narrative film, similar to that of Orin Goode and Paulie Carbone, functions to provide Danny (and the audience who identifies with Danny) a coming-of-age which neither St. Albans nor Danny's bullying colleagues can provide.

After Danny and Thandiwe meet during a social between St. Albans and Cirencester College, they exchange innocent but loving kisses and become, in spirit, *the other.* Danny falls in love with Thandiwe's intellect and her African body. Now, his coming-of-age requires that he mentally resist the "already existing" (neo)colonial discourses on the African as the essential primitive. He pages through images of primitive black people visually and satirically linked to deep dark jungles. He travels through these images as if descending into a

BLACK WOMEN AND INTERRACIAL LOVE ■ 117

whitened hellish pit of colonized territory. Danny must negotiate previous images of and about blackness, so he can better understand the new
image of Africa as posited in Thandiwe Adjewa. Fanon explains,

> To understand something new requires that we make our-
> selves ready for it, that we prepare ourselves for it; it entails
> the shaping of a new form.[2]

Danny repents in a voice-over narrative and recounts how periodi-
cals, Tarzan comics, and Hollywood movies limited his knowledge of
blacks and Africa. Western media confined blacks to a jungle mise-en-
scene that keeps people like Paulie, Danny, Orin, and Thandiwe visually and psychologically hungry for alternative images that question,
refute, and resist racism, nationalism, and colonialism. Their desires
and actional, as opposed to reactional, moves permit forms of the
postNegritude. Danny mournfully speaks of this hunger in his voice-
over narrative: "When I started thinking about Africa, I realized the
only images I knew were from old annuals, Tarzan comics, and Hollywood movies. Cannibals with bones through their noses. Lions tarrying
the threads out of antelopes." His thoughts come to an abrupt end when
a classmate enters the room and announces that, "Embling has a letter
from his girlfriend, Lubber Lips."

The name "Lubber Lips" refers to imagined thickness and elastic-
ity of the facial lips of Thandiwe and all black folk. The word also expresses the general assumption that black women are "Lubber Lip"
thick with an unbridled elastic sexuality. Excluding Danny and his intellectual friend, the St. Albans males revel in this insensitive game.
They open and read aloud the contents of Thandiwe's letter while
Danny resigns himself to passive acceptance of their communal pleasure. Later, Danny grows weary with their games and his previous passivity wanes as a St. Albans bully prepares to take a picture of the
Cirencester girls who are changing their clothes in an adjoining room.
First, Danny tells the boy not to take a picture but his request is ignored, so he wrestles the boy to the floor. His first combative actions
lead to an organized boxing match between Danny and his opponent,
the best boxer at St. Albans. The boy blackens Danny's eye and bruises
his head. Happily, Danny wins the respect of both boxer and peers because he fought bravely.

Danny's beating recalls the beating Paulie receives from his Italian
American teenage peers who forbid him to date Orin. The taboo against

Figure 30. Danny Embling (Noah Taylor) and Thandiwe Adjewa (Thandie Newton) are boarding-school lovers in John Duigan's *Flirting*

romantic expressions across racial lines threatens the mythical boundaries of race, nation, and, in the case of interracial homosexual love, gender. Unlike Paulie, Danny wins the respect of his white male peers because this film subgenre permits alternatives to the dominant "jungle fever" discourse of the policing agents in *Jungle Fever* and *Flirting*.

Flirting explores the coming-of-age of a white young man whose encounter with a black young woman has been temporarily postponed. After they have made love in a rural motel, they are awakened by St. Albans and Cirencester college administrators—the institutional policing agents. Thandiwe and Danny geographically take separate paths but their love continues in epistolary exchanges. Their good-byes have sociopolitical significance:

> Thandiwe: "You keep this half of the world going."
> Danny: "You look after the other."

Danny is no longer confined to Tarzan comics and Hollywood fictions when he thinks about Africa. In an interpolated narrative, he reveals a better understanding of contemporary Africa and is aware of the political struggle that threatens Thandiwe's life and lasting peace in Uganda. In reflecting on Thandiwe and the effects of a dying colonialism, he confesses, "I realized that she didn't have any idea of what she had gone back to." His words introduce a visual documentary of the real dangers that awaited the Adjewa family upon their return to Uganda. The black and white newsreel footage shows African civil unrest. Images of death and violence invade a once-romantic cinematic space.

In reading the paper, Danny learns that Thandiwe's father has been executed and, from Thandiwe's letter, he discovers that her stepmother is missing. Thandiwe writes of the British-trained General Idi Amin Dada, the ruthless Ugandan leader who was responsible for the deaths of countless Ugandan citizens. Thandiwe's weekly bulletins mysteriously stop. The last black and white newsreel images show black soldiers using the butts of their rifles to break into a car holding Thandiwe and others. The screen fades to a sorrowful deep blue.

Danny's familiar image in a barren outback town appears. He describes Africa's political unrest and decries the West's political apathy as a generalized ether "that surrounds this world, washing over us all the time." He and Thandiwe had formerly reputed this apathy when it appeared in their respective boarding schools. Danny explains,

> After I was expelled, I went back home and worked in my dad's pub. I was a bit like a sleepwalker. The old town hardly seemed real anymore. I spent my time writing to embassies and government ministers. Even the Prime Minister. But mostly, I concentrated. An ether surrounds this world, washing over us all the time. And all sorts of messages get transmitted through it.
>
> I had this dread that suddenly, one day I'd know she had gone. I spent most of the time worrying her to be all right. . . . Love, I suppose. That word neither of us had used because we're both too cool for that.

Thandiwe, in voice-over narrative, reads her most recent letter to Danny. As if reading his previous thoughts, Thandiwe's letter soothes his fears and provides a poetic closure to a film that began with Danny's voice-over narrative. She writes,

Danny, we're in Nairobi now and finally safe. A lot of things have happened. I am very different, I think, from how I was when you last saw me. But I am waiting until the time when we will be able to sit down together and look into each other's eyes again. I look forward to that time and what I am going to say.

To summarize, Danny has been expelled from St. Albans and returns to his rural Australian hometown. Thandiwe Adjewa returns to a civil war-torn Uganda only to bear witness to the assassinations of her father and the disappearance of her stepmother. Then the Uganda police arrest Thandiwe and her siblings. Luckily, Thandiwe and her siblings find refuge in Kenya, the country of her deceased biracial mother whose identity, like that of Thandiwe, is both European and African. The two teenage lovers exchange letters that bridge their geographical distance and create philosophical oneness. Their correspondence does not reflect Proustian remembrances of their boarding school past; nor are they idealistic guarantees of a better world to come. Their words merely express a vision of a better world and a will to pursue it. Together, their thoughts complement the other and express an international sociopolitical commitment that is so often lacking in most dramatizations of interracial love. Their chance meeting and closing words express the possibility of fruitful transnational, transracial alliances. Such alliances have also been alluded to in the poetry of Bob Kaufman and in the characters Orin Goode and Paulie Carbone in Lee's *Jungle Fever*. Danny, a rural white Australian boy, and Thandiwe, a cosmopolitan black Ugandan girl, have matured by their meeting. They eagerly await the return to their poignant but brief romance. For the most part, *Flirting* is directed at the teenage market even though it received an R rating.

WHAT A DIFFERENCE THE CHOICE OF SEX MAKES

Flirting presents a black woman in a transracial relationship that disturbs exclusionary racial and masculinist narratives. Such narratives would have women attached to same-race but different-sex mates. Transracial and other postNegritude forms of empowerment contest monolithic identity formation and permit inventive narratives that are dreamt as well as lived in real time. The films mentioned in this chapter might appear to be less sexually transgressive than images of interracial same-sex intimacy as dramatized in Lizzie Borden's *Born in Flames* (1983), Isaac Julien's *Young Soul Rebels* (1991), and Maria Maggenti's *The Incredibly True Adventures of Two Girls in Love* (1995). Still, the filmic depiction of middle-class, heterosexual, interracial love represents a form of sexual transgression, since it must negotiate and resist racist social conventions. The love that dare not seek its filmic representation delegitimizes race-based patriarchal ordering systems that also deny *sustained* same-sex unions. I emphasize the word "sustained" because assimilationist efforts will forgive those who repent their prior interracial and homosexual intimacies. The past racial and/or sexual transgressions are excused as long as the offense is not repeated. There is no hierarchy of transgression in postNegritude because such acts are not solely done to *épater les bourgeois*.

Consequently, the films tend to support a worldview in which the sharing of similar values binds individuals regardless of their race, ethnicity, and nationality. Similar to the shortsightedness of the integrationist and the equally limiting alternative, the race-conscious nationalist, these films do not and perhaps cannot provide truths about the complexities of life in the postNegritude; they can only dramatize its tensions without guarantees. The films do not respond to ethnic cleansing in Eastern Europe and Africa or the increasing racial and antiSemitic violence (against Jews and Arabs) in Western Europe and the United States. This all leads me to believe that intraclass rivalries will create those necessary postNegritude tensions that concurrently attract and repel the most unlikely candidates. These people will continue to form sustained friendships that are occasionally intimate. Their spiritual family will continue to pose the necessary questions and, from Negritude time to postNegritude time, seek answers.

CONCLUSION WITHOUT ANY GUARANTEE

In "Negritude to PostNegritude," I described how American popular culture reproduces monolithic images of black sexuality. This second chapter also showed how certain types of black creativity resist and simultaneously assimilate essentialist racial and sexual notions about identity. The convergence of postNegritude and Negritude acts-of-knowing produces intraracial tension that generates the possibility of an extraracial alliance with nonblacks. For example, the gay and women's

Figure 31. Anni Domingo and Joseph Charles in Sankofa's *Passion of Remembrance*. Photo by David A. Bailey.

movements sometimes function as a safe house for black women, gays, and lesbians who would not suppress their desires for equality within the black liberation movements of the sixties and seventies. In this light, a film of interest is Maureen Blackwood and Isaac Julien's film *Passion of Remembrance* (1986), which portrays racism in Britain and homophobia and sexism in the Black British community.

By forming multiracial unions with progressive, moderate, and conservative groups, people have created interracial, transnational, and cross-gender coalitions. Black participation in such unions is not always evoked by racial concerns or even what I have discussed as postNegritude concerns. Likewise, this book has its analytical limits which determine the breadth of my postNegritude analysis and its discussion of certain types of art. Still, the principal goal of this work remains applying postNegritude analysis to black art in order to interpret its *images* that occasionally resist monolithic representations and narrow-minded views on black subjectivity.

"Black Masculinity of the Negritude" and "Renegotiating Black Masculinity" explained how certain black films, literature, and photographs construct masculinity and racial identity in a postNegritude manner. In both chapters, I analyzed different assumptions about racial, gender, and sexual identity in the black community. "Black Masculinity of the Negritude" compared the treatment of racial and gender issues in two male-authored novels, one female-authored play, and the poetry of a biracial poet. All four black artists wrote during the Black Arts literary period when black nationalist sentiments dominated black creative production and consumption. "Renegotiating Black Masculinity" examined the creative work of two black gay artists whose art resists forms of black masculinity that would ignore or dehumanize their equally valid homosexual identity.

In an effort to trace the unending struggle to articulate a postNegritude vision, I have limited my analysis to a few exceptional works that were produced after 1960. This study has focused on particular black diasporic creations in an effort to first show how postNegritude philosophical and theorctical paradigms were present and active during the heyday of the Black Arts and black nationalist movements of the mid-1960s. Admittedly, postNegritude was, at that time, not widely celebrated by black cultural taste makers. Nevertheless, the womanist and transracial writings of certain black artists, such as John A. Williams, Ayi Kwei Armah, Adrienne Kennedy, and Bob Kaufman, intervened to condemn the *many* faceted acts of racial, sexual, and religious discrimination.

This book has discussed how black artists imaginatively deconstruct monolithic forms of black subjectivity. Throughout this work, there has been a sustained argument for an open-ended blackness that tolerates and learns to appreciate womanists, gays, lesbians, and multiracial people. The postNegritude dramatizes these groups as they struggle against ignorance that breeds distrust and fear of what is considered foreign, immoral, and disloyal.

NOTES

1. POSTNEGRITUDE AND CRITICAL THEORY

1. Frantz Fanon, *Black Skin, White Masks*, trans. Charles Lam Markman (New York: Grove Weidenfeld, 1967), p. 192. Further references to this work will be cited as *Black Skin*.
2. Ibid., p. 192.
3. Ibid., p. 193.
4. Ibid., p. 191.
5. My analysis recognizes that the production of culture and the production of identity are more imaginary than concrete. I also recognize that these imaginary processes are connected to the world economy which concretely determines how culture and identity are produced by multinational corporations. See my analysis of Spike Lee's *Malcolm X* for further discussion of these limits of black cultural production within multinational corporations like Time-Warner Incorporated.
6. Fanon, *Black Skin*, p. 154.
7. Ibid. pp. 172–73.
8. Stuart Hall, "Cultural Identity and Diaspora," in *Identity: Community, Culture, Difference*, ed. Jonathan Rutherford (London: Lawrence and Wishart, 1990), p. 223. All further references to this article will be cited as "Cultural Identity." Hall writes,

> There are at least two different ways of thinking about 'cultural identity'. The first position defines 'cultural identity' in terms of one, shared culture, a sort of collective 'one true self', hiding inside the many other, more superficial or artificially imposed 'selves', which people of a shared history and ancestry hold in common. . . . This 'oneness', underlying all the other, more superficial differences, is the truth, the essence . . . of the black experience. It is this identity which a . . . black diaspora must discover, excavate, bring to light and express.
>
> Such a conception of cultural identity played a critical role in all the post-colonial struggles. . . . It lay at the centre of the vision of the poets of 'Negritude' . . . and of the Pan-African political project, earlier in the century.

9. Hall, "Cultural Identity," p. 222.
10. Pierre Bourdieu, *In Other Words: Essays Towards a Reflexive Sociology* (Stanford, Calif.: Stanford University Press, 1990), p. 31. All further references to this text will be cited as *In Other Words*.
11. Elaine H. Kim, "Defining Asian American Realities Through Literature," in *The Nature and Context of Minority Discourse*, ed. Abdul R. JanMohamed and David Lloyd (New York: Oxford University Press, 1990), p. 147.
12. Mark A. Reid, *Redefining Black Film* (Berkeley, Calif.: University of California Press, 1993), p. 113. Here, the term *postNegritude* refers to any *action*, as opposed to *tension*, that creates, reveals, and/or exposes the nonessentialist nature of black cultural identity because it is socially constructed and reconstructed. It is not biologically given. PostNegritude actional purposes can result in the visual and literary arts as well as any sociopolitical activism that produces and safeguards an open-ended, creative dialogue between subcultures, insiders, outsiders, and diverse factions.
13. Jake Lamar, *Bourgeois Blues: An American Memoir* (New York: Penguin Books, 1992), pp. 95–96.
14. Hall, "Cultural Identity," pp. 231–32.
15. Ibid., p. 222.
16. Ibid., p. 225. Also see bell hooks, *Black Looks: Race and Representation* (Boston: South End Press, 1992), p. 5. Here hooks borrows the same quotation to describe the ongoing political process of resis-

tance and "to critically interrogate old narratives, suggesting alternative ways to look at blackness, black subjectivity, and, of necessity, whiteness." My use of this particular quotation describes the difference between Negritude and postNegritude, indicates generational shifts in black diasporic cultural production, and affirms the folding and unfolding process of any construction of identity.

17. Bourdieu, *In Other Words*, p. 37.
18. Barbara Christian, "The Race for Theory," in *The Nature and Context of Minority Discourse*, ed. Abdul R. JanMohamed and David Lloyd (New York: Oxford University Press, 1990), p. 47.
19. Michele Wallace, *Invisibility Blues: From Pop to Theory* (New York: Verso Press, 1990), p. 215.
20. Reid, *Redefining Black Film*, p. 4.
21. Caren Kaplan, "Deterritorializations: The Rewriting of Home and Exile in Western Feminist Discourse," in *The Nature and Context of Minority Discourse*, ed. Abdul R. JanMohamed and David Lloyd (New York: Oxford University Press, 1990), p. 364.
22. Ibid., p. 354.
23. Fanon, *Black Skin*, p. 229.
24. Ibid., p. 191. See chapter 1, note 4.
25. "After O.J. and the Farrakhan-led Million Man March: Is Healing Possible?" *Tikkun* 10, no. 6 (November/December, 1995): 12–20.

2. NEGRITUDE TO POSTNEGRITUDE

1. Homi K. Bhabha, "The Third Space: Interview with Homi Bhabha," in *Identity: Community, Culture, Difference*, ed. Jonathan Rutherford (London: Lawrence and Wishart, 1990), p. 216.
2. Fanon, *Black Skin*, p. 188.
3. Pratibha Parmar, "Black Feminism: the Politics of Articulation," in *Identity: Community, Culture, Difference*, ed. Jonathan Rutherford (London: Lawrence and Wishart, 1990), p. 110.
4. Ibid., p. 110.
5. Bhabha, "The Third Space," p. 216.
6. Fanon, *Black Skin*, p. 222.
7. Ibid., p. 160.
8. The photograph entitled Man in Polyester Suit (1980) appears in Robert Mapplethorpe, *Black Book* (New York: St. Martin's Press, 1986), p. 55.

9. Roland Barthes, *Mythologies* (New York: Hill and Wang, 1972), pp. 151–52.
10. Ibid., p. 152.
11. Ibid.
12. W. Lawrence Hogue, *Discourse and the Other*, p. 24.
13. Malcolm X, *By Any Means Necessary: Speeches, Interviews, and a Letter by Malcolm X*, ed. George Breitman (New York: Pathfinder Press, 1970), p. 118.
14. Clayborne Carson, *Malcolm X: The FBI File*, with an introduction by Spike Lee, ed. David Gallen (New York: Carroll and Graf Publishers, Inc., 1991), pp. 42–43.
15. Cornel West, "A Matter of Life and Death," *October* 61 (Summer 1992): 23. West argues,

> As long as we simply hide various particularizes . . . there cannot be a radical democratic project. So there must be strategies and tactics that cut across identity politics, cut across region, and gender, race, and class. Class is still around even though it's been unable to constitute an identity that has the saliency and potency of the other identities. And we must attempt to think about how we create and sustain organizations that acknowledge this. Because we're in the bind we're in partly because we've been unable to generate the transgendered, transracial, transsexual orientation of social motion, social momentum, social movement. And if we can't do that, then there will be many, many more David Dukes by the end of the twentieth century, even while we engage in our chatter about identity.

16. Abdul R. JanMohamed and David Lloyd, "Towards a Theory of Minority Discourse," introduction to *The Nature and Context of Minority Discourse*, ed. Abdul R. JanMohamed and David Lloyd (New York: Oxford University Press, 1990), pp. 13–14.

3. BLACK MASCULINITY OF THE NEGRITUDE

1. Stuart Hall, "Cultural Identity," p. 223. See note 8 of chapter 1 for the full quotation from Hall's article.

2. Simon Mpondo, "From Independence To Freedom: A Study of the Political Thinking of Negro-African Writers in the 1960's," (Ph.D. diss., University of Washington, 1971), p. 1.
3. Mpondo, p. 2.
4. Fanon, *Black Skin*, p. 188.
5. Michel Foucault, *The Order of Things: An Archaeology of the Human Sciences* (New York: Vintage Books, 1973), p. 328.
6. Mpondo, p. 1.
7. Houston A. Baker Jr., *Modernism and the Harlem Renaissance* (Chicago: The University of Chicago Press, 1987), p. 50.
8. Henry Louis Gates Jr., *The Signifying Monkey: A Theory of Afro-American Literary Criticism* (New York: Oxford University Press, 1988), p. xxvi.
9. John A. Williams, *The Man Who Cried I Am* (Boston: Little Brown, 1967; rpt. New York: Thunder's Mouth Press, 1985), pp. 338–39.
10. Ibid., p. 102.
11. Ibid., p. 186.
12. Gates, *The Signifying Monkey*, p. 130.
13. Mpondo, p. 2.
14. Ayi Kwei Armah, *Fragments* (New York: Macmillan Company, 1969), p. 274.
15. Ibid., p. 275.
16. Ibid., p. 283.
17. Bhabha, "The Third Space," p. 213.
18. Adrienne Kennedy, "Funnyhouse of a Negro" in *Adrienne Kennedy in One Act* (Minneapolis: University of Minnesota Press, 1988), p. 4.
19. Ibid., p. 23.
20. Ibid., p. 6.
21. Ibid.
22. Ibid.
23. Ibid., p. 19.
24. Ibid., p. 17.
25. Ibid., p. 21.
26. Ibid., p. 23.
27. Ibid.
28. Marc Robinson, *The Other American Drama* (New York: Cambridge University Press, 1994), p. 127.

29. Ibid., p. 128.
30. Biographical note on Bob Kaufman in Sarah L. Prakken, ed., *The Reader's Adviser: A Layman's Guide to Literature*, vol. 1, 12th ed. (New York: R.R. Bowker Company, 1974), p. 322.
31. Maria Damon, *The Dark End of the Street: Margins in American Vanguard Poetry*,(Minneapolis: University of Minnesota Press, 1993), p. 33.
32. James A. Page, *Selected Black American Authors: An Illustrated Bio-Bibliography* (Boston: G.K. Hall & Co., 1977), p. 150. In the biographical piece on Kaufman, there is a quotation from the *Poetry of Black America* by Arnold Adoff.
33. Tony Seymour, "Don't Forget Bob Kaufman," *San Francisco Examiner*, 25 April 1976, section 35, p. G5.
34. James Boyer, "Towards Print," *Trace*, 26 (April 1958): 1–5.
35. Biographical note on Bob Kaufman in Ann Evory, ed., *Contemporary Authors*, vols. 41–44, first revision (Michigan: Gale Research Company, 1979), p. 362.
36. Bob Kaufman, "San Francisco Beat," in *Solitudes Crowded With Loneliness* (New York: New Directions, 1965), p. 31.
37. Arthur Knight and Kit Knight, *The Beat Book* (San Francisco: *Unspeakable Visions of the Individual*, 1974), p. 174.
38. Tony Seymour, "Don't Forget Bob Kaufman," *San Francisco Examiner*, 25 April 1976, section 35, p. G5.
39. Tom Moran, "The Reemergence of a Streetside Survivor from the Bay Beatnik Era," *Los Angeles Times*, 4 October 1981, sec. BKS, p. 3, col. 4.
40. Bob Kaufman, "Oct. 5th, 1963," *Golden Sardine* (San Francisco: City Lights Books, 1967), p. 80.
41. During the 1960s the nation witnessed the murder of Medgar W. Evers, John F. Kennedy, Malcolm X, and Dr. Martin Luther King.
42. The fire-bombing took the lives of four young African American girls.
43. Bob Kaufman, "Benediction" in *Solitudes Crowded With Loneliness* (New York: New Directions, 1965), p. 9.
44. Ibid.
45. Jeffrey Dahmer was a serial killer who ate his dead black male victims. Dahmer was later murdered by an inmate.
46. Kaufman, "Benediction."

47. Ibid.
48. Jean Toomer, "Brown River, Smile," in *American Negro Poetry*, ed. Arna Bontemps (New York: Hill and Wang, 1963), pp. 34–35.
49. Bob Kaufman, "Believe, Believe," in *Golden Sardine*, p. 48.
50. Ibid.
51. Ibid.
52. Toomer, "Brown River, Smile," p. 37.
53. Bob Kaufman, "Second April," in *Solitudes Crowded With Loneliness*, p. 66.

4. RENEGOTIATING BLACK MASCULINITY

1. Miriam Hansen, in *Camera Obscura* 20/21 (May-September, 1989), p. 172. In discussing film and spectatorial relations, Hansen argues, "we need to grant the 'ordinary' female viewer a certain interpretive capability, a reflective distance in relation to the roles she is expected to assume. For one thing, there is a *hermeneutic* trajectory, discontinuous and problematic as it may be, which links the critic with both the past empirical viewer and the hypothetical spectator insofar as both the historical horizon of reception and textual positions of address are critical constructs. . . . both depend on the critic's conscious and unconscious mediation. . . . More specifically, conceptualizing an alternative tradition requires a concept of *experience* which not only is the opposite of socially constructed signs and systems of representation but, rather, mediates between individual perception and social determinations, and emphatically entails memory and an awareness of its historical diminishment.
2. Alice Walker, *In Search Of Our Mothers' Gardens: Womanist Prose* (New York: Harcourt Brace Jovanovich, 1983), pp. xi–xii.
3. *The American Heritage Dictionary of The English Language*, 3rd ed. (New York: Houghton Mifflin Company, 1992), p. 1446.
4. Jacques Lacan, *Ecrits: A Selection*, trans. Alan Sheridan (New York: W. W. Norton & Company, 1977), p. 172.
5. Joseph Bristow, "Being Gay: Politics, Identity, Pleasure," *New Formations* 9 (Winter 1989): 61.
6. Mark A. Reid, "Dialogic Modes of Representing Africa(s): Womanist Film," *Black American Literature Forum* 25 (1991): 377.

7. Ibid., p. 378.
8. Many of Mapplethorpe's black male nudes that I discuss appear in Robert Mapplethorpe, *Black Book* (New York: St. Martin's Press, 1986).
9. Richard Marshall, *Robert Mapplethorpe/Richard Marshall* (New York: Bulfinch Press, 1990), pp. 208–10.
10. A copy of Thomas and Dovana (1987) appears in *Robert Mapplethorpe/Richard Marshall*, p. 180.
11. Ibid., p. 88.
12. Mapplethorpe, *Black Book*: see Derrick Cross (1983), p. 2; Ron Simms (1980), p. 6; Rick (1980), p. 8; Ajitto (1981), p. 10; Bob Love (1979), p. 13; Jack Walls (1982), p. 53; Untitled (1980), p. 54; and especially Man in Polyester Suit (1980), p. 55.
13. Rotimi Fani-Kayode, "Traces of Ecstasy," *Ten.8*, no. 28 (1988): 42.
14. Alex Hirst, interview with author. London, England, 27 June 1991.
15. Fani-Kayode, "Traces of Ecstasy," p. 36.
16. Teshome H. Gabriel, "Theses on Memory and Identity: In Search of the Origin of the River Nile," *Emergences* I (Fall 1989): 134.
17. Leni Riefenstahl, *The Last of the Nuba* (New York: Harper and Row, 1974).
18. Fani-Kayode, "Traces of Ecstasy," p. 39.
19. Fanon, *Black Skin*, p. 170.
20. A photograph of Baker in her banana dress appears in Phyllis Rose, *Jazz Cleopatra: Josephine Baker in Her Time* (New York: Doubleday, 1989), p. 117.
21. Sander L. Gilman, "Black Bodies, White Bodies: Toward an Iconography of Female Sexuality in Late Nineteenth-Century Art, Medicine, and Literature," *Critical Inquiry* 12 (Autumn 1985): 212–13.
22. Mapplethorpe, *Black Book*: George Bradshaw (1980), p. 22.
23. Melody D. Davis, *The Male Nude in Contemporary Photography* (Philadelphia: Temple University Press, 1991), p. 81.
24. Ibid. Also see Janine Chassequet-Smirgel, *Creativity and Perversion* (New York: W. W. Norton and Company, 1984), pp. 98–99.
25. Davis, *Male Nude*, p. 81.
26. Sander L. Gilman, p. 213.
27. Fani-Kayode, "Traces of Ecstasy," p. 41.
28. Ibid. p. 39.

29. Trinh T. Minh-Ha, "Of Other Peoples: Beyond the 'Salvage' Paradigm," in *Discussions In Contemporary Culture*, ed. Hal Foster, no. 1 (Seattle: Bay Press, 1978), p. 138.
30. Cornel West, "Black Culture and Postmodernism," in *Remaking History*, Discussions in Contemporary Culture, ed. Barbara Kruger and Phil Mariani, no. 4 (Seattle: Bay Press, 1989), p. 89.
31. This photograph is a homoeroticized fantasy and contrasts with Rotimi's photographs of Togolese fishermen in Lome and Nigerian fishermen in Lagos which are published in Rotimi Fani-Kayode, *Black Male/White Male* (London: GMP Publishers Ltd., 1988), pp. 12–15.
32. Mapplethorpe, *Black Book*: Man in Polyester Suit (1989), p. 55.
33. In the brochure *A Retrospective: Rotimi Fani-Kayode, Photographer (1955-1989)*, The Black-Art Gallery, London, England, 20 June–27 July 1991.
34. Kobena Mercer, "Looking For Trouble," *Transition* 51 (1991): 191.
35. Ibid., p. 192.
36. Isaac Julien and Kobena Mercer, "True Confessions: A Discourse on Images of Black Masculinity," *Ten*. 8, no. 22 (1986): 5.
37. *Photography/Politics Two*, ed. Pat Holland, Jo Spence, and Simon Watney (London: Comedia/Methuen, 1987). A revised version of "Imagining the Black Man's Sex" appears in the British anthology *Male Order: Unrapping Masculinity*, ed. Rowena Chapman and Jonathan Rutherford (London: Lawrence and Wishart, 1988), pp. 141–53.
38. Julien and Mercer, "True Confessions," p. 6.
39. Robert Stam, "Bakhtin, Eroticism and the Cinema: Strategies for the Critique and Trans-Valuation of Pornography," *CineAction!* (Fall 1987): 20.
40. Fanon, *Black Skin*, p. 177. In commenting on the West's epic narrative of black sexuality, Fanon explains,

> For the majority of white men the Negro represents the sexual instinct (in its raw state). The Negro is the incarnation of a genital potency beyond all moralities and prohibitions. The women among the whites, by a genuine process of induction, invariably view the Negro as the

keeper of the impalpable gate that opens into the realm
of orgies, of bacchanals, of delirious sexual sensations.
. . . Reality destroys all these beliefs. But they all rest on
the level of the imagined, in any case on that of a
paralogism.

5. BLACK WOMEN AND INTERRACIAL LOVE

1. Cornel West, *Race Matters* (Boston: Beacon Press, 1993), p. 73.
2. Fanon, *Black Skin*, p. 95.

BIBLIOGRAPHY

Alburquerque, Klaus de. "Daughters of the Dust: The Making of an American 'Classic'." *Reconstruction* 2, no. 2 (1993): 122–25.

Appiah, Kwame Anthony. *In My Father's House: Africa in the Philosophy of Culture.* New York: Oxford University Press, 1992.

Armah, Ayi Kwei. *Fragments.* New York: The Macmillan Company, 1969.

Baker Jr., Houston. *Modernism and the Harlem Renaissance.* Chicago: University of Chicago Press, 1987.

Barthes, Roland. *Mythologies.* Trans. Annette Lavers. New York: Hill and Wang, 1972.

Baudrillard, Jean. *Cool Memories, 1 and 2: 1980–1990.* Paris: Editions Galilee, 1987 and 1990.

Bayles, Martha. "Malcolm X and the Hip Hop Culture." *Reconstruction* 2, no. 2 (1993): 100–103.

Belsey, Catherine. *Critical Practice.* New York: Methuen, 1980.

Bhabha, Homi K. *The Location of Culture.* New York: Routledge, 1994.

Bontemps, Arna, ed. *American Negro Poetry.* New York: Hill and Wang, 1963.

Bourdieu, Pierre. *Outline of a Theory of Practice.* Trans. Richard Nice. New York: Cambridge University Press, 1977.

———. *In Other Words: Essays Towards a Reflexive Sociology.* Trans. Matthew Anderson. Stanford: Stanford University Press, 1990.

Bradley, David. "Malcolm's Mythmaking." *Transition* 56 (1992): 20–46.

Breitman, George, ed. *By Any Means Necessary: Speeches, Interviews, and a Letter by Malcolm X.* New York: Pathfinder Press, 1970.

Bristow, Joseph. "Being Gay: Politics, Identity, Pleasure." *New Formations* 9 (Winter 1989): 61–81.

Carson, Clayborne. *Malcolm X: The FBI File*. With an introduction by Spike Lee. New York: Carroll and Graf Publishers, Inc., 1991.

Chapman, Rowena, and Jonathan Rutherford, eds. *Male Order: Unrapping Masculinity*. London: Lawrence and Wishart, 1988.

Chassequet-Smirgel, Janine. *Creativity and Perversion*. New York: W. W. Norton and Company, 1984.

Clay, Mel. *Jazz-Jail and God: Bob Kaufman*. San Francisco: Androgyne Books, 1987.

Damon, Maria. *The Dark End of the Street: Margins in American Vanguard Poetry*. Minneapolis: University of Minnesota Press, 1993.

Dash, Julie. *Daughters of the Dust: The Making of an African American Woman's Film*. New York: The New Press, 1992.

Davis, Melody D. *The Male Nude in Contemporary Photography*. Philadelphia: Temple University Press, 1991.

Davis, Mike. *City of Quartz: Excavating the Future in Los Angeles*. London: Verso, 1990. Reprint, New York: Vintage Books, 1992.

Delany, Samuel R. *The Motion of Light in Water: Sex and Science Fiction Writing in the East Village, 1957–1965*. New York: Arbor House/William Morrow, 1988.

———. *Silent Interviews*. Hanover, N.H.: Wesleyan, 1994.

Ekpo, Denis. "Towards a Post-Africanism: Contemporary African Thought and Postmodernism." *Textual Practice* 9:1 (Spring 1995): 121–35.

Fani-Kayode, Rotimi. *Black Male/White Male*. London: GMP Publishers Ltd., 1988.

———. "Traces of Ecstasy." *Ten.8* 28 (1988): 36–43.

———. *A Retrospective: Rotimi Fani-Kayode, Photographer (1955–1989)*. London: The Black-Art Gallery, 1991.

Fanon, Frantz. *Black Skin, White Masks*. Trans. Charles Lam Markman. New York: Grove Weidenfeld, 1967.

Foucault, Michel. *The Order of Things: An Archaeology of the Human Sciences*. New York: Pantheon Books, 1971. Reprint, New York: Vintage Books, 1973.

Funderberg, Lise. *Black, White, Other: Biracial Americans Talk about Race and Identity*. New York: William Morrow, 1994.

Gabriel, Teshome. "Theses on Memory and Identity: In Search of the Origin of the River Nile." *Emergences* 1 (Fall 1989): 131–37.

Gates Jr. Henry Louis. *The Signifying Monkey: A Theory of Afro-American Literary Criticism*. New York: Oxford University Press, 1988.
———. "Hybridity Happens." *Village Voice Literary Supplement* (October 1992): 26–27.
Gilman, Sander. "Black Bodies, White Bodies: Toward an Iconography of Female Sexuality in Late Nineteenth-Century Art, Medicine, and Literature." *Critical Inquiry* 22, no. 2 (Autumn 1985): 204–42.
Gilroy, Paul. *There Ain't No Black in the Union Jack: The Cultural Politics of Race and Nation*. London: Unwin Hyman, 1987.
———. "Nothing But Sweat inside my Hand: Diaspora Aesthetics and Black Arts in Britain." *Black Film/British Cinema*. ICA Documents no. 7. London: Institute of Contemporary Arts, 1988: 44–46.
———. *Small Acts: Thoughts on the Politics of Black Cultures*. London: Serpent's Tail, 1993.
———. *The Black Atlantic: Modernity and Double Consciousness*. Cambridge, Mass.: Harvard University Press, 1993.
Hall, Stuart. "Cultural Identity and Diaspora." In *Identity: Community, Culture, Difference*, ed. Jonathan Rutherford, pp. 222–37. London: Lawrence and Wishart, 1990.
———. "New Ethnicities." In *Black Film/British Cinema*, ICA Documents no. 7, pp. 27–31. London: Institute of Contemporary Arts, 1988.
Hansen, Miriam. "Individual Response." *Camera Obscura* 20/21 (May-September 1989): 169–74.
Haug, Wolfgang Fritz. *Commodity Aesthetics, Ideology and Culture*. New York: International General, 1987.
Henriques, Julian. "Realism and the New Language." In *Black Film/British Cinema*, ICA Documents no. 7, pp. 18–20. London: Institute of Contemporary Arts, 1988.
Hirst, Alex. Interview with author. London, England, 27 June 1991.
Hogue, W. Lawrence. *Discourse and the Other*. Durham: Duke University Press, 1986.
Holland, Pat, Jo Spence, and Simon Watney, eds. *Photography/Politics Two*. London: Commedia/Methuen, 1987.
hooks, bell. *Black Looks: Race and Representation*. Boston: South End Press, 1992.
Jameson, Fredric. *The Geopolitical Aesthetic: Cinema and Space in the World System*. Bloomington: Indiana University Press, 1992.

JanMohamed, Abdul R. and David Lloyd, eds. *The Nature and Context of Minority Discourse.* New York: Oxford University Press, 1990.

Jones, Bill T. "Sculpture in Flight: A Conversation with Bill T. Jones." *Transition* 62 (1993): 188–202.

Judy, Ronald A.T. "The New Black Aesthetic and W. E. B. Du Bois, or Hephaestus, Limping." *Massachusetts Review* 35:2 (Summer 1994): 249–82.

Julien, Isaac and Kobena Mercer. "True Confessions: A Discourse on Images of Black Masculinity." *Ten.8* 22 (1986): 4–8.

Kaufman, Bob. *Solitudes Crowded With Loneliness.* New York: New Directions, 1965.

———. *Golden Sardine.* San Francisco: City Lights, 1967.

———. *The Ancient Rain: Poems 1956-1978.* New York: New Directions, 1981.

———. *Cranial Guitar: Selected Poems by Bob Kaufman.* Edited by Gerald Nicosia. Minneapolis: Coffee House Press, 1996.

Kellner, Douglas. *Media Culture: Cultural Studies, Identity and Politics between the Modern and the Postmodern.* New York: Routledge, 1995.

Kennedy, Adrienne. "Funnyhouse of a Negro" in *Adrienne Kennedy in One Act*, pp. 1–23. Minneapolis: University of Minnesota Press, 1988.

———. *People Who Led to My Plays.* New York: Alfred A. Knopf, 1987.

Knight, Arthur and Kit Knight. *The Beat Book.* San Francisco: Unspeakable Visions of the Individual, 1974.

Lacan, Jacques. *Ecrits: A Selection.* Trans. Alan Sheridan. New York: W. W. Norton & Company, 1977.

LaCapra, Dominick, ed. *The Bounds of Race: Perspectives on Hegemony and Resistance.* Ithaca: Cornell University Press, 1991.

Laclau, Ernesto. "Universalism, Particularism, and the Question of Identity." *October* 61 (Summer 1992): 83–90.

Lamar, Jake. *Bourgeois Blues: An American Memoir.* New York: Penguin Books, 1992.

Lee, Spike. "Generation X: A Conversation with Spike Lee and Henry Louis Gates." *Transition* 56 (1992): 176–90.

Lyotard, Jean-Francois. *The Postmodern Explained: Correspondence 1982–1985.* Minneapolis: University of Minnesota Press, 1992.

Mapplethorpe, Robert. *Black Book.* New York: St. Martin's Press, 1986.

Marshall, Richard. *Robert Mapplethorpe/Richard Marshall.* New York: Bulfinch Press, 1990.

McClintock, Anne. *Imperial Leather: Race, Gender and Sexuality in the Colonial Contest.* New York: Routledge, 1995.

Mercer, Kobena. "Looking For Trouble." *Transition* 51 (1991): 184–97.

———. "Back To My Roots: A Postscript on the 80s." *Ten.8* 2, no. 3 (Spring 1992): 32–39.

Morrison, Toni, ed. *Race-ing Justice, En-gendering Power: Essays on Anita Hill, Clarence Thomas, and the Construction of Social Reality.* New York: Pantheon Books, 1992.

Mpondo, Simon. "From Independence To Freedom: A Study of the Political Thinking of Negro-African Writers in the 1960's." Ph.D. diss., University of Washington, 1971.

Nielsen, Aldon Lynn. *Reading Race: White American Poets and the Racial Discourse in the Twentieth Century.* Athens: University of Georgia Press, 1988.

Perry, Bruce. *Malcolm: The Life of a Man Who Changed Black America.* Barrytown, N.Y.: Station Hill Press, Inc., 1991.

Reid, Mark A. "Dialogic Modes of Representing Africa(s): Womanist Film." *Black American Literature Forum* 25, no. 2 (Summer 1991): 375–88.

———. "The Photography of Rotimi Fani-Kayode." *Wide Angle* 14, no. 2 (1992): 38–51.

———. *Redefining Black Film.* Berkeley: University of California Press, 1993.

———. "The Brand X of PostNegritude Frontier." *Film Criticism* 22, nos. 1–2 (Fall/Winter, 1995): 17–25.

Riefenstahl, Leni. *The Last of the Nuba.* New York: Harper and Row, 1974.

Robinson, Marc. *The Other American Drama.* New York: Cambridge University Press, 1994.

Rose, Phyllis. *Jazz Cleopatra: Josephine Baker in Her Time.* New York: Doubleday, 1989.

Rutherford, Jonathan, ed. *Identity: Community, Culture, Difference.* London: Lawrence and Wishart, 1990.

Said, Edward W. "The Politics of Knowledge." *Raritan* 2, no. 1 (Summer 1991): 17–31.

Stam, Robert. "Bakhtin, Eroticism and the Cinema: Strategies for the Critique and Trans-Valuation of Pornography." *CineAction!* (Fall 1987): 13–20.

Stoler, Ann Laura. *Race and the Education of Desire: Foucault's History of Sexuality and the Colonial Order of Things.* Durham, N.C.: Duke University Press, 1995.

Stone, Alan A. "The Taming of Malcolm X." *Reconstruction* 2, no. 2 (1993): 93–99.

Trinh, T. Minh-Ha. "Of Other Peoples: Beyond the 'Salvage' Paradigm." In *Discussions in Contemporary Culture 1,* ed. Hal Foster, pp. 138–41. Seattle: Bay Press, 1987.

Walker, Alice. *In Search of Our Mothers' Gardens: Womanist Prose.* New York: Harcourt Brace Jovanovich, 1983.

Walker, Clarence E. *Deromanticizing Black History: Critical Essays and Reappraisals.* Knoxville, Tenn.: University of Tennessee Press, 1991.

Wallace, Michele. *Invisibility Blues: From Pop to Theory.* New York: Verso Press, 1990.

Ware, Vron. *Beyond the Pale: White Women, Racism and History.* London: Verso, 1992.

West, Cornel. "Black Culture and Postmodernism." *Discussions in Contemporary Cultures 4,* ed. Barbara Kruger and Phil Mariani, pp. 87–96. Seattle: Bay Press, 1989.

———. "A Matter of Life and Death." *October* 61 (Summer 1992): 20–23.

———. *Race Matters.* Boston: Beacon Press, 1993.

Williams, John. "Recreating Their Media Image: Two Generations of Black Women Filmmakers." *Cineaste* XX, 3 (1994): 38–41.

Williams, John A. *The Man Who Cried I Am.* Boston: Little Brown, 1967. Reprint, New York: Thunder's Mouth Press, 1985.

Wood, Joe, ed. *Malcolm X: In Our Own Image.* New York: St. Martin's Press, 1992.

INDEX